The Silver & Gold Investor's Profit Guide

Where to get the best prices on the best silver & gold investments

By
Daniel Rosenthal
and Ellen Young

 ISBN: 0-938689-02-9

The Institute for the Preservation of Wealth, Inc.

Introduction

Stop throwing your money away with overcharging, price-gouging silver and gold dealers. Don't waste another dollar. Put your wallet away. Then read this survey and learn which of these dealers...

* Have the worst prices for silver. Plus which have the best.

* Which dealers have the worst prices for gold -- and which give you the best.

* Which are the rudest. The reports about one dealer were so bad, we phoned them ourselves, posing as naive investors. We were DISGUSTED.

* Which tried to high-pressure our callers into investments they didn't want.

* Which dealers SGR does NOT recommend -- regardless of price -- and why.

PLUS...

* How to avoid getting scalped on double eagles. Some dealers charge 4 times, 8 times -- and sometimes more than 10 times -- the mark-up

on the same quality double eagles as other dealers.

* The only two ways to buy with complete safety against dealer default. The problems at Deak & Co. show that even the cleanest and best-intentioned dealers can get into trouble.

* 4 guidelines that will help you save big dollars every time you buy silver and gold.

* How to buy direct from a major wholesaler and get the same price Investment Rarities or Deak would get. This is NOT the phony "at spot" or "wholesale" ads you see in the paper. It's for real. On large purchases, buy from this huge bullion concern -- and save thousands of dollars.

* How to save as much as $12 per maple leaf, 70¢ per ounce of silver, and $554 per bag of US silver coins (pre-1965) by shopping at the right dealer.

Table of Contents

Part I: The dealers

1. Stop wasting hundreds -- or thousands -- of dollars every time you buy silver and gold

If you're like most investors, you're probably paying bloated mark-ups -- double, sometimes triple what you need to -- every time you buy silver and gold. You get the same maple leafs, the same US silver coins, double eagles, and silver and gold bullion -- but you pay hundreds of dollars more than you have to. You probably don't even realize it.

Indeed, a maple leaf averaged $339 at Silver Towne. But if you'd bought the exact same maple leaf at MTB, you would have paid $351 -- an extra 3.9%. On a large order of 20 coins, that added up to an extra out-of-pocket cost of $248.

A kilo bar of gold averaged $10,933 at First National Monetary. That's a full $369 more than the very same kilo bar purchased at Medlar's Coins.

Those price spreads are bad enough. But when we priced the US silver coins, it got much worse. At Lee Numismatics, you could have purchased a bag of US silver coins (pre-1965, $1,000 face value) for $5,212.

The same bag of silver coins purchased at Western Monetary Consultants would have cost you $5,766 -- an extra $554 (10.6%).

If you were buying 1,000 ounces of the handy, investor-sized 100-ounce bars, you would have paid $426 more at Fiscal & Monetary -- that's 6.4% -- than if you bought the identical bars from Silver Towne.

But by far the two most shocking and disgusting price spreads between dealers were on US $20 gold double eagles (St. Gaudens, A-Mark graded and guaranteed) and US silver-clad Kennedy half dollars.

On the double eagles, the difference between the worst-priced and the best-priced dealer was $119.90 per coin -- a full 15%.

The price spread on the US silver-clad Kennedy half dollars was even greater -- a huge 29%. IPMC (the worst-priced dealer) was charging an incredible $1.90 per ounce more than Security (the best-priced dealer).

On the sell side, the savings were also impressive.

The biggest difference was for the $1000 bags of US silver coins. The amount you'd receive varied sharply, ranging from your best price at Silver Towne, who offered $4042, to the Medlar and Colonial offers of $3667 each.

This means that by selling your bag of silver coins to Silver Towne, instead of Colonial or Medlar, you could walk away from the transaction with an extra $375 -- or 10.2% more money in your pocket. The difference with silver at $5.06 an ounce translates to your having enough money left over after dealing with Silver Towne to buy an additional 74 ounces of silver. That's worth the trouble of learning what you're doing in the marketplace.

Both Camino and Security quoted us top prices of $527 each for our Engelhard 100-ounce silver bar. This compared with a bottom-of-the-barrel quote from Western Monetary Consultants of $495. The difference here between who you sell to translates into an extra $32 or 6.5% per bar.

In terms of percentages, the competition over who had the best bid for maple leafs provides the smallest price differential in our survey, a spread of only 3% between Silver Towne at the top and Western Monetary Consultants at the bottom. That 3% may not sound like much, but WE would feel infinitely better about selling

a maple leaf and getting $11 more for it at one dealer than losing those 11 bucks to some other dealer. On the maple leafs we priced out, that came to $110.

So, stop wasting your hard-earned money. You can save 10%, 20% -- sometimes even 30% -- every time you buy silver and gold. And to get the best price, you do NOT have to sacrifice either safety or service. Indeed, in our own purchases, we've found that some of the lower-priced dealers offer the best service.

How this survey was conducted

The tables in this issue show the results of SGR's price survey of US silver and gold dealers. We conducted our buying survey on November 6, November 12, and November 18, 1985. The Comex spot price for silver was $6.09, $6.08, and $6.09 on each day, respectively. The Comex spot price for gold was $324.65, $324.40, and $323.70 on each day, respectively.

The sell side of the survey was conducted on July 8, July 9, and July 10, 1986. Comex spot prices each day

during our survey averaged as follows: $5.12, $5.08, and $5.07 for silver and $348, $348, and $347 for gold, respectively.

The price quotations shown in the tables are averages of the dealer prices over the three-day periods.

Clearly, when you're buying silver and gold, what counts is the total price you pay; what counts when you're selling is the total amount of the check you receive. So, in our tables, we've shown the net price you would have paid, including commissions, delivery charges on the buy side, and any other miscellaneous fees. Sales tax was not included.

We didn't include shipping charges when selling because of the wide potential variation in costs based upon where customers and dealers are located. A bag of $1000 face-value US silver coins weighs 55 pounds and shipping charges could easily wipe out one dealer's apparent edge over another, depending on distance. So bear this in mind when using the information we've gathered for you.

Our calls were anonymous and were done by us with every effort to appear as legitimate potential customers. The data in this report, plus our calculations, are correct

to the best of our knowledge. Errors, however, are always possible, so we are unable to provide any absolute guarantee of accuracy.

We also wish to stress that we didn't actually buy or sell any silver and gold to these dealers. The information in this report is based upon what these dealers and their sales representatives told us over the phone which may or may not represent actual company policies and/or prices. We welcome letters from readers who find discrepancies between what we were told and what actually transpires in your account.

2. The worst-priced and best-priced dealers for buying silver bullion

For this edition of the survey, we priced out two types of silver bullion purchases: (a) a thousand ounces in the form of a 1,000-ounce bar and in the form of ten 100-ounce bars; (b) bags of US silver coins (pre-1965) and the US silver-clad Kennedy half dollars.

The worst-priced dealer we surveyed for silver was clearly Western Monetary Consultants. They gave us the very worst prices on bags of US silver coins (pre-1965) and the next to worst prices on silver bullion and bags of Kennedy halves.

We attended a Western Monetary seminar last spring. Bill Kennedy, President of Western Monetary, told us, with refreshing openness, that he thought he was the highest-priced dealer in the country. If we heard of a higher-priced dealer, he wanted to know about it so he could raise his price.

Well, Bill, the time may be at hand. IPMC is giving you a good run for your money. They were the second-worst-priced dealer for silver -- and close on the heels of Western Monetary. Deak was the third-worst-priced

dealer, but significantly less expensive.

Fiscal & Monetary Services doesn't deal in the Kennedy halves, so we couldn't compare them, directly, to the 3 other highest-priced dealers. However, they had the worst prices on 100-ounce bars of silver bullion and the second worst on 1,000 ounce bars.

On the other hand, the three best-priced dealers -- who were very close to one another -- were:

- Best prices -- Silver Towne
- Second best -- Monex
- Third best -- Security Rare Coins

Lee Numismatics and Benham were virtually in a dead heat for fourth place, behind them.

The spread between the best and the worst-priced dealers was surprising, even to us. Deak was, on the average, 9.8% more expensive than Silver Towne; IPMC was 11.4% higher; and Western Monetary was 12.8% higher.

2. The worst and best-priced for buying silver bullion

Buying ten 100-ounce silver bars

Dealer Ranking	Dealer Ask Price	Survey Leader* vs. Other Dealers $ Savings
***1. Silver Towne**	**$6,577****	—
2. Norcap	6,590	$ 13
3. Colonial	6,598	21
4. Sunshine	6,606	29
5. Blanchard	6,650	73
6. Shearson	6,660**	83
7. Camino	6,675	98
8. Republic	6,690	113
9. Benham	6,703	126
10. C. Rhyne	6,713	136
11. Monex	6,714**	137
12/13. Lee Numismatics	6,749	172
12/13. MTB	6,749	172
14. Auric	6,760	183
15. First National	6,773	196
16. Gold Standard	6,779	202
17. Western Federal	6,787	210
18. Security	6,793	216
19. Sam Sloat	6,807	230
20. IPMC	6,844	267
21. Newcastle	6,868	291
22. Medlar's	6,897**	320
23. Deak-Perera	6,909	332
24. Investment Rarities	6,928	351
25. Western Monetary	6,940	363
26. Fiscal & Monetary	7,003	426

Buying one 1,000-oz. silver bar

Dealer Ranking	Dealer Ask Price	Survey Leader* vs. Other Dealers $ Savings
***1. Shearson**	**$6,252**	—
2. Camino	6,327	$ 75
3. Silver Towne	6,365**	113
4. Colonial	6,408	156
5. Monex	6,426	174
6. Republic	6,507**	255
7. Sunshine	6,518	266
8. Auric	6,675	423
9. Fiscal & Monetary	6,843	591
10. Western Monetary	6,953	701

** Two-day average, not three. In some instances our callers couldn't get through. In others, they got through, but couldn't get a quotation.

2. The worst and best-priced for buying silver bullion

Buying a bag of US silver coins (pre-1965, $1,000 face value)

Dealer Ranking	Dealer Ask Price	Survey Leader* vs. Other Dealers $ Savings
*1. Lee Numismatics	$5,212	—
2. Silver Towne	5,227	$ 15
3. Monex	5,270	58
4. Security	5,279	67
5. Sam Sloat	5,290	78
6. Benham	5,320	108
7. IPMC	5,331	119
8. Investment Rarities	5,353	141
9. Blanchard	5,355	143
10. Colonial	5,367	155
11. Norcap	5,368	156
12. MTB	5,394	182
13. Medlar's	5,408	196
14. Western Federal	5,426	214
15. Shearson	5,431	219
16. C. Rhyne	5,435	223
17. Auric	5,437	225
18. Newcastle	5,460	248
19. Camino	5,480	268
20. Fiscal & Monetary	5,532	320
21. First National	5,552	340
22. Deak-Perera	5,567	355
23. Republic	5,599	387
24. Western Monetary	5,766	554

Buying a bag of US silver-clad Kennedy half dollars ($1,000 face value)

Dealer Ranking	Dealer Ask Price	Survey Leader* vs. Other Dealers $ Savings
*1. Security	$1,894	—
2/3. Monex	1,904	$ 10
2/3. Silver Towne	1,904	10
4. Republic	1,969	75
5. Benham	1,978	84
6. Investment Rarities	1,986	92
7 Lee Numismatics	1,993	99
8. Sam Sloat	2,003	109
9. Colonial	2,021	127
10. C. Rhyne	2,030	136
11/12. Blanchard	2,040	146
11/12. Norcap	2,040	146
13. Camino	2,047	153
14. First National	2,049	155
15. Western Federal	2,054	160
16. MTB	2,078	184
17. Newcastle	2,093	199
18. Auric	2,095	201
19. Medlar's	2,108	214
20. Deak-Perera	2,253	359
21. Western Monetary	2,352	458
22. IPMC	2,450	556

3. The worst-priced and best-priced dealers for buying gold bullion

On gold bullion, we priced out krugerrands, maple leafs, and gold kilo bars.

On the average, the 4 worst-priced dealers were MTB, IPMC, Auric, and Investment Rarities, in that order. Also among the worst-priced were Western Monetary and Western Federal. But because neither carried gold kilo bars, we couldn't include them in our weighted averages.

The 3 best-priced dealers were Silver Towne, Medlar's Coins, and Republic. Their prices were "only" a few percent lower than the worst-priced. But on a $24,000 purchase that "only" translated into as much as $616 of savings.

3. The worst and best-priced for buying gold bullion

Buying one gold kilo bar*** (32.15 ounces)

Dealer Ranking	Dealer Ask Price	Survey Leader* vs. Other Dealers $ Savings
***1. Medlar's**	**$10,564**	—
2. Republic	10,574**	$ 10
3. Silver Towne	10,579	15
4. Benham	10,586	22
5. Camino	10,607	43
6. Colonial	10,643	79
7. Newcastle	10,684	120
8. Norcap	10,686	122
9. MTB	10,689	125
10. Shearson	10,696	132
11. Deak-Perera	10,698	134
12. C. Rhyne	10,701	137
13. Auric	10,716	152
14. IPMC	10,736	172
15. Investment Rarities	10,801	237
16. Monex	10,824	260
17. First National	10,933	369

**Two-day average, not three. In some instances our callers couldn't get through. In others, they got through, but couldn't get a quotation.

***Security was not included in this table because on one day we couldn't get a price, and on the second day they gave us an obviously erroneous price. We were left with only one price to judge from.

Buying maple leafs (20 coins)

Dealer Ranking	Dealer Ask Price	Survey Leader* vs. Other Dealers $ Savings
***1. Silver Towne**	**$6,780**	—
2. Medlar's	6,804	$ 24
3. Republic	6,806	26
4. Colonial	6,807	27
5. Lee Numismatics	6,810	30
6. Monex	6,818	38
7. Security	6,829	49
8. Benham	6,831	51
9/10. Camino	6,833	53
9/10. First National	6,833	53
11. Sloat	6,862	82
12. Newcastle	6,864	84
13. C. Rhyne	6,884	104
14. Norcap	6,885	105
15. Deak-Perera	6,888	108
16. Investment Rarities	6,891	111
17. Auric	6,902	122
18. Blanchard	6,911	131
19. Fiscal & Monetary	6,933	153
20. Shearson	6,937	157
21. Western Federal	6,938	158
22. Western Monetary	6,961	181
23. IPMC	6,982	202
24. MTB	7,028	248

3. The worst and best-priced for buying gold bullion

Buying krugerrands (20 coins)

Dealer Ranking	Dealer Ask Price	Survey Leader* vs. Other Dealers $ Savings
***1. Silver Towne**	**$6,606**	—
2. Medlar's	6,613	$ 7
3. Security	6,632	26
4. Lee Numismatics	6,633	27
5/6. First National	6,634	28
5/6. Republic	6,634	28
7. Colonial	6,643	37
8. Benham	6,656	50
9. Monex	6,662	56
10. Camino	6,672	66
11/12. Investment Rarities	6,690	84
11/12. C. Rhyne	6,690	84
13. Norcap	6,691	85
14. Newcastle	6,707	101
15. Sloat	6,720	114
16. Shearson	6,744	138
17. Blanchard	6,753	147
18. Western Federal	6,760	154
19/20. Auric	6,768	162
19/20. Fiscal & Monetary	6,768	162
21. IPMC	6,794	188
22. Western Monetary	6,807	201
23. MTB	6,864	258

4. How to avoid getting scalped on gold double eagles

Traditionally, the mark-up on numismatics is much higher than on bullion. That's because the dealer theoretically has to spend a lot of time and care on grading and checking for counterfeits when he buys. That costs money.

However, in the past year-and-a-half a new product has become popular in the market: A-Mark guaranteed double eagles. A-Mark grades and certifies the coins; encases them in a tamper-proof package; and guarantees the authenticity and quality of every coin they sell.

The key benefit of the A-Mark guarantee is it makes double eagles fungible, i.e., interchangeable with one another. They're almost as easy to buy and sell as bullion. Dozens of dealers will buy them at that grade -- as long as A-Mark remains in business to back the guarantee. While it isn't perfect because you can't verify the authenticity of the coins yourself without breaking the seal -- and thus voiding the guarantee -- it's a great benefit for investors who are numismatically naive.

Because of the interchangeability of these coins, we expected the price difference to be about the same as

a maple leaf. But we were shocked and disgusted to see that the spread was actually a huge 15.2% -- a full $119.90 per gold double eagle.

The 4 worst-priced dealers on A-Mark guaranteed US double eagles were Newcastle, IPMC, Western Federal, and Blanchard, in that order.

Benham Certified Metals was clearly in a class of its own. They only charge a 1% mark-up over their cost. The other three best-priced dealers -- Lee Numismatics, Medlar's and Republic -- were significantly behind Benham. Their prices were from 2.7% higher to 3.9% higher.

Buying A-Mark Guaranteed St. Gaudens, MS 60, double eagles (10 coins)

Dealer Ranking	Dealer Ask Price	Survey Leader* vs. Other Dealers $ Savings
***1. Benham**	**$7,884****	—
2. Lee Numismatics	8,100**	$ 216
3. Medlar's	8,123	239
4. Republic	8,193	309
5. Fiscal & Monetary	8,433**	549
6. C. Rhyne	8,684	800
7. Blanchard	8,800	916
8. Western Federal	8,895	1,011
9. IPMC	9,006	1,122
10. Newcastle	9,083	1,199

**Two-day average, not three. In some instances our callers couldn't get through. In others, they got through, but couldn't get a quotation.

To see how this translates into dollars, if you bought 10 of these lovely coins at Benham, it would have cost

$7,884. At Newcastle it would have been $9,083 -- a whopping $1,199 more.

We tried to buy the A-Mark Guaranteed US $20 gold double eagles from Camino Coins. On the first day of our survey, the broker we spoke with said he could get them for us, but gave a mediocre price. On the second day, however, the owner, Burt Blumert, told our caller: "Try Investment Rarities or Blanchard if you want a guarantee."

5. C. Rhyne defends huge price differences on US gold double eagles

"Dear Dan:

"I understand your position as champion of the consumer, but I have a bone to pick with you, my friend.

"In particular, you said, 'we were shocked and disgusted to see that the spread (on A-Mark Guaranteed double eagles) was actually a huge 15.7%...' You stated that 'because of the interchangeability of these coins we expected the price difference to be about the same as a maple leaf.'

"Come on, Dan. You should know better. Or at least you should ask some questions before vilifying good dealers.

"There are excellent reasons why the mark-up on rare coins, including A-Mark Guaranteed gold coins, is higher than for maple leafs or bullion.

"1. The main reason is that a dealer cannot hedge his rare coin inventory like he can on bullion.

Bullion, unlike rare coins, can be easily resold into the wholesale market on an immediate basis so that the dealer has no risk when the price moves.

"In order that a dealer have rare coins in stock for customers to look at, he is at risk on the unsold coins when the market changes. Most dealers sell at the current prevailing market, so they have to have sufficient mark-up on a coin to absorb any possible decline in that individual type of rare coin.

"2. The Rare Coin Market has a life of its own, independent of the bullion markets. And the various individual rare coins within the market also have independent performance characteristics.

"*For example*: A-Mark Guaranteed U.S. $20 St. Gaudens, MS-60 condition, peaked March 23, 1984 with a dealer cost of $946.00. Why would they be so expensive when Gold Bullion was only $386.25 that day? The reason was that $20 St. Gaudens had been promoted heavily by major coin dealers and that many newsletters at that time were reporting that new IRS dealer reporting regulations were

excluding rare coins.[1] This had caused a relative 'buying spree' on U.S. $20 St. Gaudens, which are favorites for investors.

"After a few weeks, the coins came down in price, then went up, then came down, etc. In fact, since that peak, the A-Mark Guaranteed U.S. $20 St. Gaudens went down to $629.00 (dealer cost) one year later when gold spot was $292.25, before starting back up again.

"The point is that no dealer in his right mind would buy an inventory (which is necessary in order to fill orders cash and carry like you recommend) that he cannot hedge unless he has enough of a profit margin to withstand such price declines as outlined above. It is ridiculous to expect dealers to offer these coins at commission rates comparable to those charged on Maple Leaf bullion coins.

"3. As outlined earlier, the cost of doing

---

1. SGR note: It's about time that the disgusting way investors were fleeced at that time was brought out into the open (by someone other than Jim Cook and ourselves).

business is high with rare coins. It takes a lot of capital to tie up a nice selection of coins. It requires a lot of money to pay for the knowledge required (numismatists)...not to mention the cost of traveling to coin shows all over the country. Although these costs are reduced when dealing with "guaranteed gold," there are basic costs that do not go away, i.e., rare coin staffs.

"Dan, I just had the pleasure of buying a twelve-coin U.S. gold type set back from a customer. He had bought it from me two years ago and just sold it back to me for a $5,000 profit. This is a net gain of 38.5% to him. Not too shabby during a period of declining bullion prices!

"My commission when he bought the set was 15%. Believe me, I'm worth it! And so are most of the other dealers out there. On some extremely large rare coin deals, I'll go as low as 8%, but I usually charge 10% to 15% on rare coins. Most responsible dealers that have been in business for a while consider these mark-ups fair.

"A guy's got to make a decent profit considering his risk. In defense of the overwhelming majority

of dealers, 10% to 15% is a fair mark-up on rare coins, including A-mark Guaranteed Gold. And as you know by now, a 15% mark-up is not a 15% profit. That 15% mark-up on rare coins translates into a profit of less than 5% because of the inventory losses and overhead. The marketplace is motivated by profit and dealers are entitled to their fair share. Without it, the market would cease to exist."

Sincerely yours,

Craig Rhyne

Craig W. Rhyne

President

C. Rhyne & Associates

SGR responds to Mr. Rhyne

Craig is one of our favorite small dealers, and he's nailed us on errors several times in the past. But he's dead wrong on this one.

The A-Mark Guaranteed double eagles are not rare coins. They're common date. Since they're already graded and guaranteed, you don't need a numismatic staff. That's the whole point behind these coins. That's why

a normal investor who knows next to nothing about numismatics can buy A-Mark Guaranteed double eagles in comparative safety.

Furthermore, the inventory risk on minor holdings for walk-in trade is negligible. Nobody has to carry 500 coins to handle walk-in trade. It's absurd. They don't sell all that many in a month.

Even if they did sell that many, they wouldn't need nearly that many on hand because A-Mark has a fast turn-around time -- two days or less -- for shipping their orders.

The proof that what we're saying is right is in the survey. Medlar's appeared to have a 5% markup. Lee Numismatics appeared to be charging around 3% over cost. And Benham was 1%. So what's the problem? Why does another firm (not Craig's) have to charge 15%?

But look, we're not here to tell dealers how much profit they can make. We DON'T advocate price controls. If Craig wants to charge $80 more per coin than another dealer -- and if someone else wants to charge another $40 on top of that -- it's their business. But it's our business to tell you what they're doing.

The point is that if you bought from the worst-priced dealer in our survey, you would have ended up with this measly little pile.

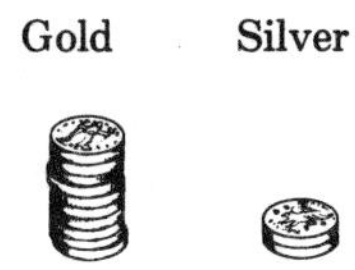

But if you bought from the best-priced dealer, you would have gotten this pile -- which has <u>154 times more silver</u>!

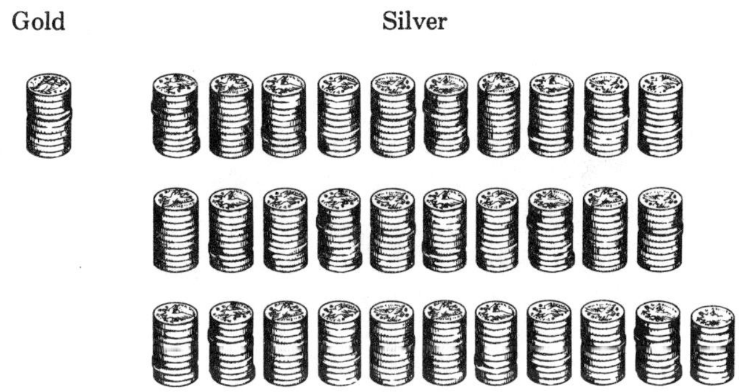

What's disgusting to us is that most investors get stuck with one of the littler piles.

6. Who had the best and worst prices when you're selling silver and gold

In this Chapter, we rate the dealers on the basis of who offers you the best prices when you're selling your silver and gold. We included three popular silver and gold investments: a 100-ounce Engelhard silver bar, a $1000 face value bag of US pre-1965 90% silver coins, and 10 maple leafs.

The dealers who offered us the highest net buy-back prices were --

Silver Towne of Winchester, Indiana, offered us the best price for our $1000 bag of silver coins.

Camino Coin Co. of Burlingame, CA, and Security Rare Coins & Bullion of Minneapolis, tied for the best price for our 100-ounce Engelhard bar of silver.

Silver Towne topped all other bidders in the competition for best offer for our 10 gold maple leafs.

Bringing up the rear by offering us the lowest prices for our silver and gold were --

Medlar's Coins of San Antonio tied with Colonial

Coins of Houston with the lowest bid for a $1000 bag of silver coins. We were surprised by the Medlar quote, as in our previous buying survey the firm finished first in buying a gold kilo bar and second in two other gold categories.

Western Monetary Consultants of Fort Collins, CO offered us the least amount of money for our 100-ounce silver bar. Western Monetary Consultants also turned in the worst bid for our 10 maple leafs.

6. The worst and best prices for selling silver and gold

SELLING
Maple Leafs (10 coins)

Dealer Ranking	Dealer Bid Price	$ Loss vs. Survey Leader*
*1. Silver Towne	$3570	—
2. Camino	3563	$ 7
3. Sam Sloat	3562	8
4. Colonial	3560	10
5. First National	3559	11
6. Lee	3545	25
7. Medlar	3540	30
8. Benham	3539	31
9. Blanchard	3538	32
10. Auric	3536	34
11. Deak	3535	35
12. Rhyne	3530	40
13. Fiscal & Monetary	3518	52
14. Security	3514	56
15/16. MTB	3511	59
Newcastle	3511	59
17. Norcap	3500	70
18. Investment Rarities	3484	86
19. Shearson	3482	88
20. Western Federal	3473	97
21. Western Monetary	3467	103

SELLING
100-oz. Silver Bar

Dealer Ranking	Dealer Bid Price	$ Loss vs. Survey Leader*
*1/2. Camino	$527	—
*Security	527	—
3. Investment Rarities	525	$ 2
4. Auric	524	3
5. Lee	522	5
6. Blanchard	521	6
7. Sam Sloat	520	7
8. Silver Towne	514	13
9. Norcap	512	15
10/11 12/13. Deak	510	17
Medlar	510	17
Newcastle	510	17
Shearson	510	17
14/15 16/17. Colonial	509	18
Fiscal	509	18
MTB	509	18
Sunshine	509	18
18/19. Benham	505	22
C. Rhyne	505	22
20. First National	501	26
21. Western Federal	496	31
22. Western Monetary	495	32

6. The worst and best prices for selling silver and gold

SELLING
Bag of US Silver Coins (pre-1965, $1000 face value)

Dealer Ranking	Dealer Bid Price	$ Loss vs. Survey Leader*
***1. Silver Towne**	**$4042**	—
2. Security	3992	$ 50
3. Norcap	3960	82
4. Monex	3958	84
5. Lee	3943	99
6. Sam Sloat	3930	112
7. Fiscal & Monetary	3900	142
8. Western Monetary	3896	146
9. Investment Rarities	3892	150
10. Benham	3886	156
11. Camino	3875	167
12. Auric	3867	175
13. Newcastle	3842	200
14. Shearson	3838	204
15. Blanchard	3833	209
16. Western Federal	3814	228
17. MTB	3787	255
18. First National	3785	257
19. Deak	3778	264
20. C. Rhyne	3737	305
21/22. Colonial	3667	375
Medlar	3667	375

7. Two private minters that are good for small purchases

Two of the dealers in our survey sell only their own products: Sunshine Bullion and Gold Standard Corp. Both these firms offer silver and gold coins at very good prices.

Sunshine Bullion. This is the retail arm of one of America's largest silver mines. They sell 10-ounce, 100-ounce, and 1,000-ounce silver bars, and the 1-ounce silver Sunshine rounds.

They were among the best-priced on 100-ounce silver bars, and their 1-ounce silver rounds -- at only 85¢ over spot -- are very competitive with other brands. Furthermore, these 1-ounce Sunshines are beautifully designed coins.

You should note that if Sunshine were to go out of business, their coins and the 10-ounce bars would likely sell at a slight discount. But their 1,000-ounce silver bars would not, because they are a "good delivery" brand on the London Metal Exchange.

Gold Standard Corp. On their silver bullion and bullion coins, they had average prices.

But they also mint gold coins with the likenesses of hard-money greats such as Dr. Friedrich Hayek, Dr. Milton Friedman, Dr. Nicholas Deak, and Colonel E.C. Harwood -- and they've recently come out with a gold coin depicting Jesus Christ. They charge 5% over spot for the 1-ounce gold coins (very reasonable) and 12% over spot for the 1/10th-ounce gold coins.

One risk with their products is that their liquidity depends entirely on Gold Standard Corp.'s continued existence. If they were to go out of business[2] the coins and bars would be harder to sell.

---

2. We have no information one way or the other about the financial condition of these companies.

8. Gold Standard Corp. coins: As liquid as krugerrands?

"Dear Dan:

"Just a note to let you know the fine service your dealer surveys provide the customer and the dealers. Also the following suggestions:

"First, no 100 ounce bar is 'good delivery.' Only 1,000 ounce industrial bars bearing an approved hallmark and registered in the confines of a Comex depository is a 'good delivery' bar. (I am glad you no longer recommend these. While we routinely deliver 1,000 ounce industrial bars, investors are quickly disillusioned when it comes time to sell. Once they take possession, they are no longer 'good delivery.')

"Moreover, your recommendation to insist on a good delivery hallmark is confusing on anything other than industrial bars. Smaller Engelhard, Johnson Matthey, and Sunshine bars are not 'good delivery' under any conditions.

"Second, no survey was conducted on what dealers

are paying for krugerrands. I find this a serious omission since investors have apparently lost over half a billion dollars since krugerrands went from premium to discount in 1985. While you consistently (and rightfully) point to the caveat that our liquidity depends on our continued existence as a private enterprise, this seems pale next to the caveat of the liquidity disfunctions created by governments. May I point out that GSC mintages are older than maple leafs and have outlived the krugerrand at least in the U.S. While you rightfully and consistently point to the inherent dangers of private coinage the very same dangers are even more apparent in government coinage. We need look no further than the krugerrand.

"I take exception that the liquidity of our coins depends 'entirely' on our continued existence. The fact that these coins are indeed gold and are what we say they are assure the same degree of liquidity as krugerrands today. (We are melting krugerrands daily.) Moreover, the magnitude of disfunction created if we go out of business is considerably less than what has been created by the combination of intervention by the South

African government and the United States government."

Cordially,

Conrad J. Braun

President

Gold Standard Corp.

SGR responds to Mr. Braun

Conrad is one of the pioneers of the gold coin industry. His firm, Gold Standard Corp., produces an interesting variety of privately minted coins that we enjoy, buy, and use as private currency.

Conrad is correct that only 1,000-ounce bars are good delivery. He is also correct in saying that our recommendation to insist on good delivery hallmarks is confusing on anything other than industrial-sized (1,000-ounce) bars.

To clarify, Engelhard and Johnson Matthey, for example, are "good delivery" brands, i.e., Comex will accept their 1,000-ounce bars in fulfillment of a futures contract. The smaller 100-ounce bars are not good delivery, but because the 1,000-ounce bars are good

delivery, the brands are famous in the trade throughout the world. Therefore, the smaller 100-ounce and 10-ounce Engelhard and Johnson Matthey bars are far more liquid than, say, a First National Monetary, Gold Standard Corp., or Silver Towne bar, each of which is essentially accepted without discount ONLY at the firm of issuance.

The point we were trying to make is this: Our readers are reporting that they are buying 100-ounce silver bars from dealers with unspecified hallmarks. They pay the going rate for brand name bars. But then, when they take delivery, they're given the house brand which sells at a discount from the Engelhard and Johnson Matthey bars. If the customer protests, they're charged extra to get the more liquid "brand name" bars. So when you buy silver, specify you want a brand name bar like Engelhard or Johnson Matthey. Insist that it be written on your confirmation slip.

Conrad's third point is that we include no buy-back prices for krugerrands. At the time of his letter, we had not finished the selling part of this survey.

Next, Conrad is wrong about the liquidity of his coins. While there was temporarily a panic about

krugerrands, and investors were induced into uneconomical switches into maple leafs, double eagles, or whatever, you can still walk into thousands of coin stores across the country and sell back krugerrands. This is NOT the case with Gold Standard Corp. coins which are unfortunately not nearly as widely known throughout the investment community. Indeed, as Conrad told us in a subsequent letter...

> "In case after case dealers turn their nose up to our products and offer to buy them back from investors at a discount...We recommend that our customers sell back only to us."

So, we stand by our point: The liquidity of Gold Standard Corp.'s silver and gold coins depends entirely on Gold Standard Corp.'s continued existence. Without Gold Standard Corp., the coins would be harder to sell.

Finally, Conrad makes a very important point that the sell-back price for krugerrands has gone from 1% over spot a few years ago to 2% below spot today. He's absolutely right. This is a risk that we've consistently warned about, most particularly in regards to the fractional gold coins, which sell at up to a 30% premium, and in regards to semi-numismatics, which have premiums

of 30%, 50% -- sometimes even 100% -- over spot. But it applies to any gold coin. The premium is entirely at risk. If something happens to put the coin out of favor -- in the case of the krugerrand, the US government intervening in the market -- the premium may disappear -- or even become a discount.

The only way you can minimize -- or eliminate -- the risk on the premium is to buy coins with as low premiums as possible. We'll show you how to do that in Part II of this Profit Guide.

9. Two dealers who tried to high-pressure our callers into investments they didn't want

At most dealers, when we called up and said we wanted to buy something, they gave us a price and let us buy it. They didn't try to pressure us into investments we hadn't asked for and didn't want.

Two of the 30 dealers, however, got consistently bad grades in this area: Security Rare Coins and International Precious Metal Corp. (IPMC).

Security Rare Coins brokers were always polite and helpful, but our callers found them too pushy and insistent about numismatics. One broker kept saying (approximately), "Why do you want to buy bullion? It's such a rotten investment."

International Precious Metals was even worse. Their brokers were, generally speaking, genuinely resistant to selling us bullion or bullion coins. They consistently tried to push our callers into either leverage programs or high-premium "semi-bullion" coins.

It's not just that they were high-pressure. With one exception, the brokers seemed, to us, misleading.

One broker, for instance, tried to sell our callers British Proof Sets, which he described as "8 pounds of gold for only $1,300!" Well, 8 pounds is over $33,000 worth of gold -- so it sounds like quite a "bargain." But the reality was that he was referring to the denomination of the coins -- not the weight.

Furthermore, posing as naive investors, we told the broker we'd been reading Ruff and Rosenthal and were interested in core holdings. The broker tried to sell us leverage -- which was totally inappropriate. He also tried to sell us the British 5 pound gold coin -- again, totally inappropriate for core holdings.

We had always considered IPMC one of the class dealers and had said so publicly and privately. But when we finished with that series of calls, we said to ourselves, "There's one firm I'd fight to keep my mother away from." The same advice goes to you.

10. Three dealers we do NOT recommend -- regardless of price

Citibank. You can't lock in a price over the phone whether you have an account with them or not. If you buy from them, you're really speculating. By the time they make your purchase, the price could be $30 higher or lower than when you checked their price.

Furthermore, they aren't set up for physical delivery. Just certificates. You have to wait until you get your certificate, and then arrange delivery. Too many hassles.

Harrison Gold & Silver Exchange. Their prices are good, but their service is ROTTEN.

International Precious Metals Corp. (IPMC). See our discussion under the section "Two dealers who tried to high-pressure our callers into investments they didn't want."

11. Four silver and gold offers to avoid --

Shell's "$20 St. Gaudens" is so small,
you need a magnifying glass to see the design

When we first saw this ad, we did a double take. "$20 St. Gaudens for only $19.90 apiece -- that can't be possible." Then we saw the catch. It's a gold miniature, NOT the real government issue. And from the looks of the picture labeled "Shown in actual size," it looks like you'd need a tweezer to pick it up. You can hardly even see the St. Gaudens design.

They say it's 24 karat gold -- but they don't tell you the weight. From the size in the picture, we estimate it has at most $7 worth of gold in it, probably no more than $5 worth, and quite likely less.

We called up Shell to try to confirm our estimate. But they told us "If it's not in the brochure, that information is not available." Then we tried to order it, so we could weigh it. But they told us we couldn't, because we weren't Shell cardholders. A friend who has a Shell card has promised to order it for us. We'll let you know.

This $19 is a small sum of money, but there's an important principle here. Whenever you see an ad for a silver and gold coin -- privately or publicly minted -- watch out if the ad doesn't tell you the weight, or if it tells you in some incomprehensible measurement like "pennyweights," "grains," or "cubits." Any such reluctance to spell out specifically what you're getting should be a big red flag.

MTB's Liberty silver coin:
Silver bullion at $29.95 an ounce!

"A Treasured Family Heirloom," boasts the ad. "This exquisite Liberty Trade Silver™ Piece is the first of its kind to be struck in over 100 years. Weighing one full troy ounce of pure .999 silver, 'Liberty In Any Language' has been struck in immaculate proof quality for discerning collectors."

The trouble is, this "Family Heirloom" is just another silver bullion coin. The only thing that sets it aside from other privately minted silver coins is its absurdly high price. Other issuers, such as A-Mark, Engelhard, Gold Standard Corp., Monex, and Sunshine sell their

bullion coins at between 85¢ and $1.50 over spot. MTB's "Liberty In Any Language" is selling at a whopping $21 over spot. We've been told liberty costs, but to us this is ridiculous.

ICC's Mex 2 peso has a higher premium than uncirculated double eagles

---

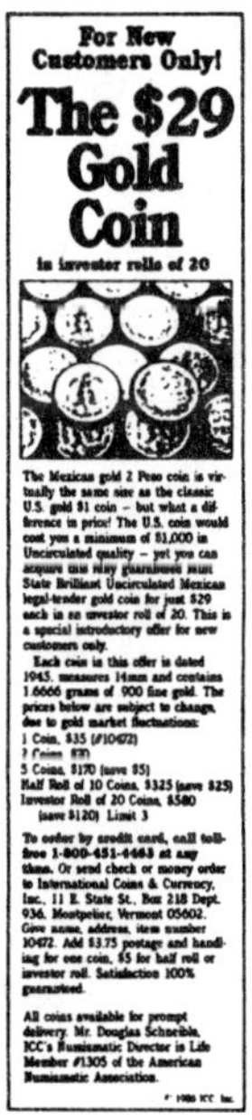

Lydia, my secretary, sniffed out this one -- which she clipped from Natural History and sent to me with the comment "Do you believe this ad?" The dealer was International Coins & Currency and they offered a Mexican gold 2 peso coin for $29 in rolls of 20 -- or $35 (+$3.75 shipping) individually.

Being an amateur collector, as soon as I read the first sentence of the ad, I knew Lydia had hit the mother lode. In that sentence, ICC compared the Mex 2 peso coin with the US gold $1. To even mention them in the same breath is absurd. The Mex 2 peso is an attractive but

common low-premium bullion coin. By contrast, the US gold $1 coin is quite scarce and often carries a numismatic premium maybe 25 times greater than the numismatic premium on a double eagle!

So I turned on my calculator, and went to work. The Mex 2 peso contains 0.0483 troy ounces of pure gold. The premium ICC is charging comes to a huge 136%. That's a larger premium than even uncirculated gold double eagles carry -- and these Mex gold 2 pesos are NOT numismatic coins as are the double eagles. So, you know it's a rotten deal.

To confirm, I called a West Coast dealer, C. Rhyne & Associates up in Seattle, and bought the same coin for $21. ICC was charging you a whopping 66% more than the going rate for individual coins.

Blanchard pricing gold in
Napoleons at $589 per ounce

Another interesting example came in the mail from our friend Jim Blanchard. That ad offered the French gold Napoleon 20 franc, a beautiful old bullion coin for

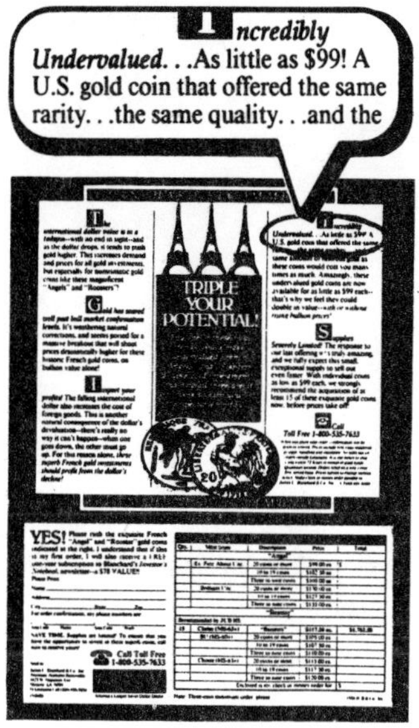

Blanchard's ad calls these coins **"Incredibly Undervalued."** But the reality is that they are way overpriced at Blanchard & Co. Our first call to another dealer showed the premium over bullion at Blanchard almost double the going rate.

$110 each. The ad -- which pictured the Napoleon the same size as the krugerrand, even though it has less than one-fifth the gold -- described them as "Incredibly Undervalued." But were they?

The Napoleon 20 franc contains 0.1867 ounces of pure gold. As a collector, I knew the coin was generally considered to be a bullion coin, and was not commonly collected by date. So I went back to my calculator and pushed a few buttons. I learned that Blanchard was pricing the gold in these bullion coins at $589 per ounce. The premium over spot came to 73.2%. That's about seven times the premium on the British gold sovereign, which is a comparable coin.

Again, a call over to C. Rhyne & Associates bought me the same coins in the same condition for $22.50 less. The premium at C. Rhyne & Associates was only 37.8%. In

other words, the premium at Blanchard & Co. is 93.6% higher than the premium at C. Rhyne & Associates.

12. Comments on the other dealers

The tables of dealer rankings in this survey are simply objective ratings of the dealer prices quoted to us. Below, we've listed some <u>subjective</u> comments about each dealer. These are based on facts we've collected and on the impressions of our anonymous callers.

<u>Auric</u>. Average prices. Mr. Aylesworth, President of Auric, has invited us down to Texas to see Auric United's operations first-hand. We've accepted verbally and are writing to him. We'll report the results in the SILVER & GOLD REPORT. In the meantime, use the same caution you would with any silver and gold dealer.

NOTE: There are still uncertainties about the Prospector Fund. Howard Ruff has written what we thought was an excellent article on the Prospector Fund in his January 20, 1986 issue of FINANCIAL SUCCESS REPORT. If you have questions about United Services or Prospector Fund, we recommend you get it. Write to FINANCIAL SUCCESS REPORT, P.O. Box 25, Pleasanton, CA 94566.

<u>Benham Certified Metals</u>. Consistently good prices and good service. The best prices on A-Mark guaranteed US $20 St. Gaudens double eagles. You can lock a price

in with Benham only if you have good funds in-house with them when you're buying, or after you've sent the metals when you're selling. However, since they have an associated money-market fund -- Capital Preservation Fund Account -- it's not a great inconvenience. Indeed, this fund is a good alternative if you want to keep some cash outside the banking system.

Blanchard. A large dealer with average to high prices. Price quotes include commissions. Although one sales person told us they "don't like to do business with non-clients," they will lock in a price over the phone. In general, quite helpful and friendly.

Brinks. They no longer sell precious metals.

Camino Coins. You can only lock in a price with this dealer if you've done business with them before. Don't assume that their good prices on bullion necessarily mean they'll have good prices on numismatics. Check around.

Colonial Coins. Good prices. Furthermore, you get a savings of 4¢ per ounce (on silver) if you pay by bank wire instead of check. Our anonymous callers always find them friendly and helpful.

Credit Suisse. We were told by Credit Suisse salespeople that they only deal in the wholesale market and will not sell to retail customers.

Deak International. They turned out rather high-priced in this survey, but their salespeople remain helpful. Deak & Co., the holding company has been sold. The people we knew best at this company, the late Dr. Nicholas Deak, Leslie Deak, and Lloyd Graavengard, are no longer there. The new management has been most cooperative with us so far. We are looking into the flow of client funds, investor safeguards, and their storage program. We'll keep you posted.

First National Monetary. Average to high prices in most categories. Good prices on krugerrands. You can lock in a price over the phone, but they tell us on large purchases they might ask for a "good faith deposit." They will buy from you only if one half of the proceeds are "reinvested" with them. Ugh!

Fiscal & Monetary Services. A small, regional, high-priced dealer. They'll lock in a price over the phone. You must send a cashier's check, certified check, or bank wire within 24 hours when you're buying, or have

the metal to them within 3 days if you're selling. That, to us, is completely fair.

Investment Rarities. We're pleased to see this normally high-priced dealer has become more competitive. Particularly since the firm's President, Jim Cook is one of the few dealers who has spoken out forcefully against the excesses in the semi-numismatic and numismatic markets.

Lee Numismatics. A new addition to our survey. They had the best prices on $1,000 bags of US silver coins (pre-1965) and the second best prices on A-Mark guaranteed double eagles. In other categories they had average to good prices.

Note: Lee is primarily a numismatic dealer. Don't automatically assume that good bullion prices will necessarily translate into good numismatic prices. Check first.

Manfra, Tordella & Brookes (MTB). A large, cash-and-carry dealer. Average to high priced. Good service. You can lock in a price over the phone.

Medlar's Coins. They are a small dealer with great prices on gold and average prices on silver. They're also

among our callers' favorite dealers -- always friendly and helpful. They'll lock in a price if you're an established customer.

Monex International. Great prices on $1,000 face value bags of US silver coins (pre-1965) and US silver-clad Kennedy half dollars. Average prices in other categories. If you're interested in leveraged silver and gold purchases, Monex has a margin program we prefer.

They also offer a bank custodial delivery program. This is a program which appears, to us, to offer investors strong safeguards without all the administrative difficulties of sight drafts. Instead of making your payment directly to Monex, you do it through an escrow account at Farmers & Merchants Bank. Farmers & Merchants releases the funds to Monex only after they've received evidence that Monex has shipped your silver and gold (usually a "notice of delivery" from Brinks).

One inconvenience in dealing with Monex is their high minimum purchase requirements: 1,000 ounces of silver, 20 ounces of gold, or a full bag of silver coins. If you just want to make a small purchase, they won't be interested.

Newcastle Financial Group. They're high-priced. As we're writing this, they are in the process of merging with the new dealer Ruffco. We're not sure how this will affect their procedures and prices, but we'll keep you posted in the SILVER & GOLD REPORT.

Norcap Financial Corp. They recently changed their name from North American Coin & Currency. Norcap had great prices on 100-ounce bars and average prices elsewhere. One disadvantage: they request your social security number before they'll lock in a price. They tell us it's kept confidential, but we think it's a disturbing invasion of your privacy.

Republic Bullion. Republic Bullion is closed, due to "depressed market conditions." Very unfortunate -- they were one of the best dealers. Republic National Bank, the parent company, will service accounts (800-223-0840). We expect you'll find higher minimums and rude service.

C. Rhyne & Associates. Average prices and very helpful brokers. You can lock in a price via a recorded conversation and wire the funds immediately, or send them good funds in advance and settle the price on the phone after it arrives.

Sam Sloat. Consistently good prices. You save $5 per 100-ounce bar if you buy 10 or more. Their salespeople make it short, sweet, and to the point.

Security Rare Coins & Bullion. New to our survey. Good prices on bullion. A little too pushy on numismatics, their main product. Don't assume that good prices on bullion automatically insures good prices on numismatics.

There's some confusion about Security Rare Coins because there are 2 entirely unrelated firms named Security Rare Coins. The firm we were referring to in the survey is located in Minneapolis. We've had consistently good dealings with them. We know nothing about the other Security Rare Coins -- which is in no way connected with Security Rare Coins in Minneapolis.

Shearson/American Express. Look in the yellow pages for your local branch. Good prices on 1,000-ounce silver bars. Average prices in other categories. You must establish an account in your local office before you can buy from them, and you'll most likely be charged sales tax.

Silver Towne. Excellent prices. Helpful service. In addition to more common hallmarks, they sell silver

bars with the Silver Towne hallmark. Be careful to specify that you don't want the Silver Towne hallmark. Insist on a good delivery brand.

Western Federal. They have average to high prices. But they provide good service, good customer safeguards, and a delivery program we prefer.

Western Monetary Consultants. Another dealer who believes you have to be high priced to survive. Their salespeople are very informative, and go out of their way to help you. For total safety, we recommend cash-and-carry or sight drafts.

Important warning

For the most part, we are not privy to the inner financial workings of the dealers in this survey. The only exceptions have been noted in other articles.

13. Dealer addresses

Auric United, P.O. Box 29568, San Antonio, TX 78229, (800) 531-7171 or (512) 696-6209.

Benham Certified Metals, 755 Page Mill Road, Palo Alto, CA 94309, (800) 447-4653 in-state and out.

Blanchard, 4425 W. Napoleon, Metairie, LA 70001, (800) 535-7633 or (504) 456-9034.

Camino Coins, 851 Burlway Road, Suite 105, Burlingame, CA 94010, (800) 348-8001 or in-state (800) 348-3001.

Colonial Coins, 909 Travis St., Houston, TX 77002, (800) 231-2392 or in-state (800) 392-4716; (713) 654-0910.

Deak International, 630 5th Avenue, New York, NY 10111, (800) 223-5510 or (212) 757-0100.

First National Monetary, First Center Office Plaza, 26913 North Western Highway, 6th Floor, Southfield, MI 48003, (800) 521-2400 or in-state (800) 551-5200; (313) 353-9770.

Fiscal & Monetary Services, 106 Congress St., Portsmouth, NH 03801, (800) 258-7322 or (603) 431-1420.

Gold Standard Corp, 1805 Grand Avenue, Kansas City, MO 64108, (800) 842-4653 or (816) 842-4653.

Investment Rarities, 1 Appletree Square, Suite 1500, Minneapolis, MN 55420, (800) 328-1860 or (612) 853-0700.

Lee Numismatics, P.O. Box 1045, 9 Sentry Way, Merrick, NH 03054, (800) 835-6000 or (603) 429-0689.

Manfra, Tordella & Brookes (MTB), 59 W. 49th St., New York, NY 10112, (800) 535-7481 or (212) 621-9502.

Medlar's Coins, 54 North Star Mall, San Antonio, TX 78205, (512) 342-5191.

Monex International, 4910 Birch St., Newport Beach, CA 92660, (800) 854-3361 or in-state (800) 432-7013; (714) 752-1400.

Newcastle Financial Group, 1815 South State Street, Suite 450, Orem UT 84058, (800) 453-1466 or (801) 224-9800.

Norcap Financial Corp, 34 West Monroe, Phoenix,

AZ 85003, (800) 528-5346 or (602) 256-5200.

C. Rhyne & Associates, 110 Cherry St., Seattle, WA 98104, (800) 426-7835 or in-state (800) 542-0824; (206) 623-6900.

Security Rare Coins & Bullion, 600 Shelard Plaza North, Minneapolis, MN 55426, (800) 328-4909 or (612) 593-0533.

Shearson/American Express, 2 World Trade Center, New York, NY 10048, (212) 321-7169.

Silver Towne, P.O. Box 424, Winchester, IN 47394, (317) 584-7481.

Sunshine Bullion, P.O. Box 214509, Dallas TX 75221, (800) 527-5769 or in-state (800) 441-2518; (214) 992-0162.

Western Federal, 8630 East Via De Ventura, Scottsdale, AZ 85258, (800) 528-3158 or (602) 998-1000.

Western Monetary Consultants, 1635 Blue Spruce Road, Fort Collins, CO 80524, (800) 525-4956 or in-state (800) 221-2144; (303) 226-3500.

Part II: The products

14. How to get an extra 8.5 ounces of pure gold every time you buy 100 ounces -- How to get an extra 20.6 ounces of pure silver every time you buy 100 ounces

---

WHAT you buy is
as important as WHERE you buy

When investing in silver and gold, you must watch what you buy as well as where you buy. You can get dramatically more silver and gold for your money every time you buy, simply by buying the right investments and avoiding the wrong ones.

For example, you could buy 100 ounces of gold bullion by investing in 425 British gold sovereigns. Under current market conditions, that would cost you $36,975. But that same $36,975 would pay for almost 111 Hungarian 100 koronas containing 108.5 ounces of pure gold. So you would get an extra 8.5 ounces of pure gold.

Alternatively, you could simply buy 100 ounces of gold in koronas, and pocket the savings -- a hefty $2,875. Either way you end up far ahead.

For silver, the differences are even more dramatic. When you buy 100 Mexican one-ounce silver libertads, the cost, as this is being written would come to $666. By contrast a 100-ounce Sunshine silver bar costs only $552. You save $114, which you could pocket, or use to purchase another 20.6 ounces of pure silver at the same unit cost.

The extra silver and gold you get is a dramatic addition to your portfolio -- it's like a free bonus you get for investing intelligently.

The philosophy of buying silver and gold bullion is simple -- if you are interested in getting the most silver and gold for your money. The object is to buy as close as you possibly can to the spot price. That means buying silver and gold investments with as low a markup as possible over bullion content.

The problem is that silver and gold investments vary widely in their markups. The markup on the Chinese panda, for example, is four times the markup on the South African krugerrand.

What we've done here is to survey the market prices of various fairly common ways of investing in silver and

gold. Then we reduced the prices of these individual investments to their per troy ounces unit prices and percentages over spot so you can easily see the best buys.

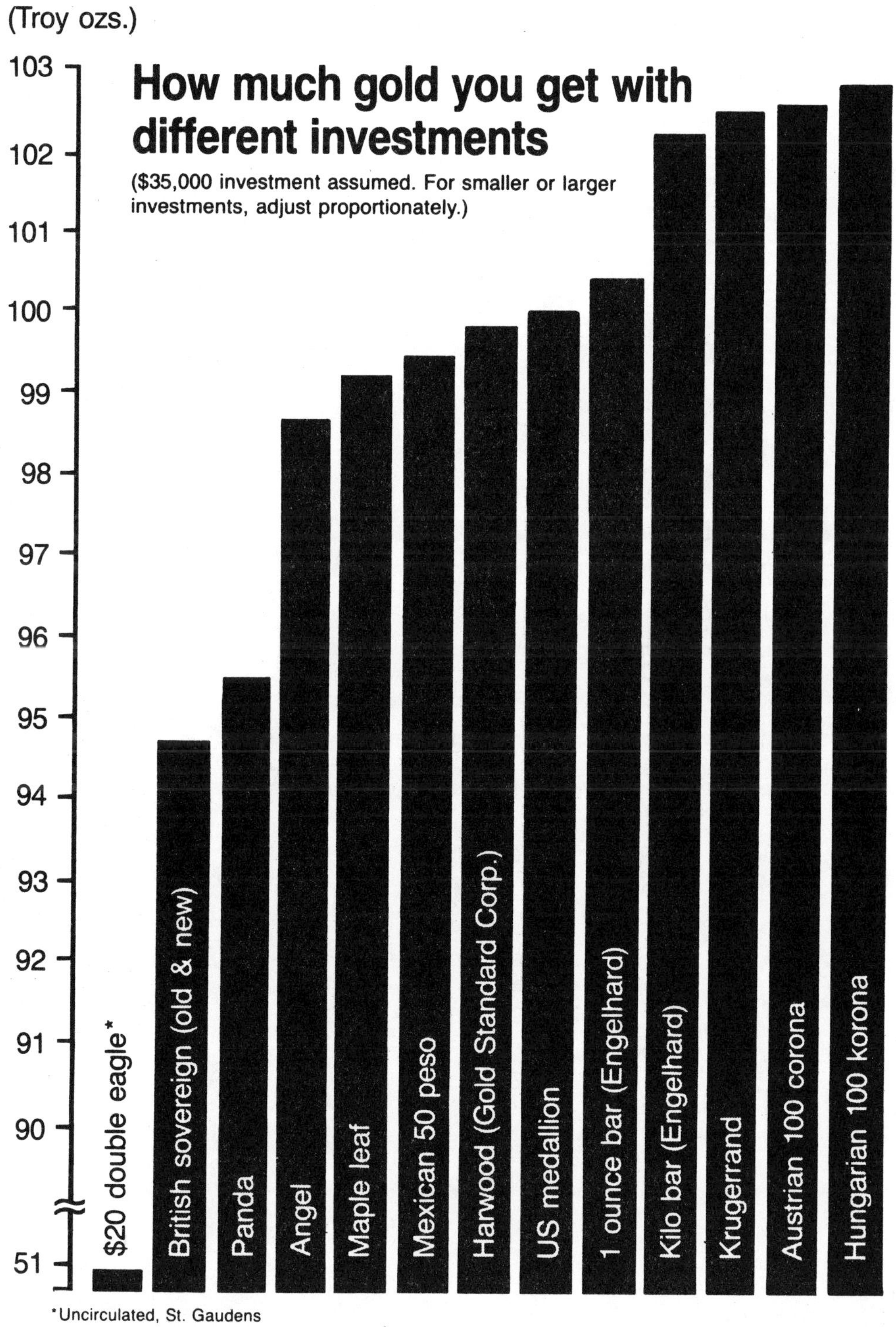

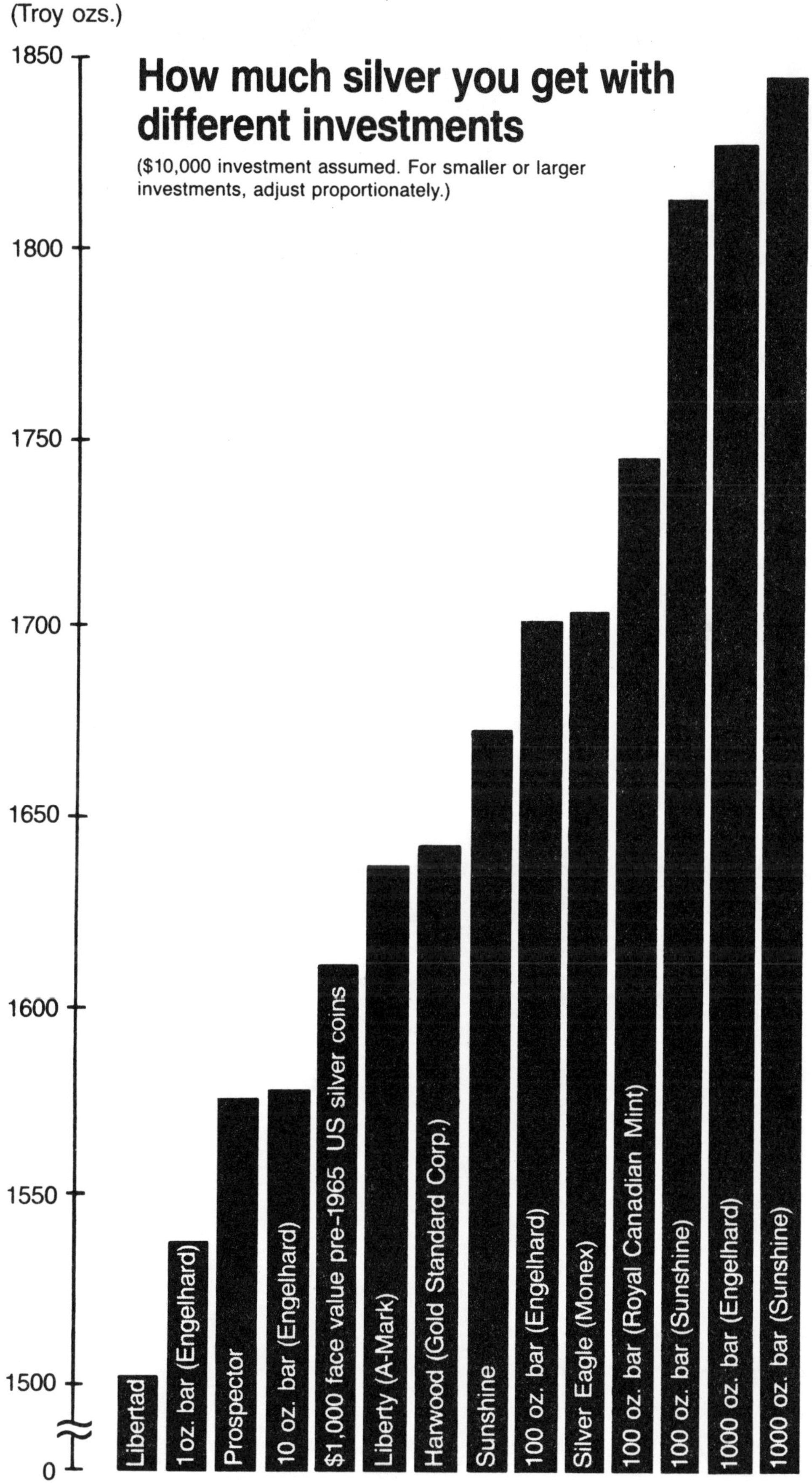
(Troy ozs.)
How much silver you get with different investments
($10,000 investment assumed. For smaller or larger investments, adjust proportionately.)
1850
1800
1750
1700
1650
1600
1550
1500
0
Libertad
1 oz. bar (Engelhard)
Prospector
10 oz. bar (Engelhard)
$1,000 face value pre-1965 US silver coins
Liberty (A-Mark)
Harwood (Gold Standard Corp.)
Sunshine
100 oz. bar (Engelhard)
Silver Eagle (Monex)
100 oz. bar (Royal Canadian Mint)
100 oz. bar (Sunshine)
1000 oz. bar (Engelhard)
1000 oz. bar (Sunshine)

15. The best buy for gold bullion

Our survey showed that the gold investment that gave you the most bullion for the dollar was the Hungarian korona. You could buy this coin for a mere 1.8% over spot. The coin contains 0.9802 ounces of pure gold and is a beautiful reminder of the Austro-Hungarian Empire.

Koronas, because of their rock-bottom premium over spot, are an absolutely super way to invest in gold bullion. One problem is they aren't as universally well known in North America as the maple leaf or the krugerrand. So, they aren't coins you should buy for your core holdings because you want maximum liquidity for that purpose.

Two other excellent buys
for gold bullion

The Austrian 100 corona and South African krugerrand followed closely on the heels of the korona. They were tied for second-best bullion buy with a premium of only 2.1% over spot. The Austrian 100 corona is the companion piece to the Hungarian 100 korona.

It's the exact same size, weight, and alloy, but has a different design. The 100 corona is more well known than its Hungarian counterpart and more liquid. Still in North America, it's unknown outside of hard-money circles, and hence, is unsuitable for your core holdings.

The once dominant bullion coin of the world, the South African krugerrand, has gone from 5.2% premium over spot in 1983 to a 2.1% premium today. The reason, of course, for this low premium is because President Reagan banned their import to the US last year. This reduced their desirability and, hence, liquidity. Still everyone knows the krugerrand today. It is synonymous in the public eye with one ounce of gold, and therefore it's extremely liquid.

At this close a premium to the spot price, there is little downside premium risk, despite what a few dealers would like you to believe.[3] We highly recommend that you take advantage of this marvelous opportunity to buy one ounce of pure gold at barely over spot price and as a suitable investment for core holdings.

3. See article on the krugerrand in the SILVER & GOLD REPORT. Vol. X, No. 12, Early July 1985. If you'd like, send a self-addressed, stamped envelope and we will send you a copy, free.

The kilo bar -- 32.15 ounces of gold -- biggest is not always best

In general, when buying almost anything, the assumption is that the more of it you buy, the less expensive it is. That's not always the case, however, as grocery consumers discovered when unit pricing was introduced. The largest jar of olives sometimes wasn't as good a buy as a smaller container. Our survey revealed a similar anomaly in the gold market. We were shocked that -- at present -- it costs less per ounce to buy any one of the common bullion coins than it does to buy a 32.15 ounce kilo bar of gold!

Still, there are pros and cons to investing in kilo bars. First the positive side. Each of the bars carries a serial number. Have your dealer record the serial number and the hallmark on your confirmation slip. File it somewhere away from where you store the bar.

If the bar is stolen, you are in much better position to deal with the insurance company by having a readily identifiable number to cite, as opposed to reporting that X number of unidentifiable coins were stolen. Also you're

in a much better position of being able to claim your property should the police ever recover it. So the serial number is a highly desirable feature of buying bars.

On the negative side, first of all, they're a relatively unattractive way to hold gold. There's nothing of beauty about a kilo bar, compared with the artistic, beautiful engravings available by buying coins. In addition, bars aren't divisible. You're stuck with 32.15 ounces in one unit. If you ever need to sell some gold, the advantages of the coins are obvious.

But the far more important problem with the kilo bar is liquidity. Dealers don't like them because they are prime candidates for counterfeiting. Coins are struck; bars are molded. It's a lot more difficult to counterfeit coins because of the engraving, dies, machinery, etc., than it is to make bogus bars that only have to be poured into molds and stamped with the refiner's hallmark, serial number, fineness, and other easily reproduced data.

The next six gold investments fall into the medium-price range

---

The next six investments in our gold survey fall into

the medium-price range -- the Engelhard one-ounce gold bar (4.2%), US one-ounce gold medallion (4.5%), the Harwood one-ounce gold coin (4.8%), the Mexican gold 50 peso (5.1%), the Canadian one-ounce gold maple leaf (5.4%), and the Isle of Man's one-ounce gold angel (6.0%).

For core holdings among these units we recommend you stay with the maple leaf. It has taken over the krugerrand's former position as the most popular gold bullion coin. It has excellent liquidity, and its premium over spot is moderate.

The maple leaf is pure gold, while all the other coins mentioned so far are made from coin alloy. This makes the maple leaf slightly more lustrous and beautiful, but it also makes it easier to scratch.

For beauty, however, we must admit that the Mexican 50 peso is one of -- if not THE -- most beautiful bullion coins ever minted. A premium of 5.1% over spot, to us, seems a mere pittance in order to acquire such an incredibly beautiful piece of gold. Wonderful gifts.

If you want to buy or sell Harwood one-ounce gold coins, you must deal with the issuers, Gold Standard Corp.

Two high-premium gold coin investments

The panda, at 9.6% over spot, is a Chinese minted one-ounce coin that has appreciated dramatically since it was first introduced in 1982. Manfra, Tordella & Brookes (MTB) in New York City is the East Coast distributor for pandas, and Panda America Corp. of Palos Verdes Estates, CA, takes care of West Coast sales. There is an active secondary market in the coins.

MTB gave us the following information --

Year	Mintage	Buy	Sell
1982	15,871	$1400	$1600
1983	22,247	900	1100
1984	27,997	675	800
1985	N/A	351	365
1986	N/A	(not on sale yet)	

Aside from the immense popularity of pandas in the US zoos, part of the reason panda coins are selling at such a high markup over spot is because of dealer promotions strongly implying that the 1985 panda and subsequent issues will appreciate in the same manner as earlier issues. We doubt this will be the case. We caution you that when you're

buying pandas, you're getting significantly less gold than you could be getting for your money and the premium on the 1985s and earlier issues could evaporate.

The British sovereigns -- both the old and the new -- three years ago carried a 9.7% premium. They're up a bit this year to 10.5%, according to our survey. There's very little downside risk on the premium for these coins (we've followed them for years). They're slightly less than one-quarter ounce of gold (0.2354/ounce). As quarter ounce gold coins go, a 10.5% premium isn't excessive.

The double eagle -- not the way to buy gold bullion

From the standpoint of being able to buy the most gold for your dollars, the single worst investment included in the survey is the US $20 double eagle. We found the double eagle (uncirculated St. Gaudens) priced at an average of 105.1% over spot.

Part of the reason for the high premium, of course, is that they haven't been minted since 1932 and are a semi-numismatic coin. Another reason is desirability. The

double eagle and the Mexican 50 peso we mentioned earlier are our two favorite gold coins. The St. Gaudens is a simply magnificent example of coin design artistry. They make wonderful gifts, but they certainly aren't the way to buy pure gold if that's your goal. You'll get less than half as much gold as you would buying Hungarian koronas, Austrian coronas or krugerrands.

The premiums of 13 popular gold investments

Rank	Unit (Spot Gold $335/Troy Ounce)	Total Weight (Troy ozs.)	Gold Fineness (Purity)	Pure Gold (Troy ozs.)	Price Per Item	Price Per Troy oz.	Percent Over Spot Price
1.	Hungarian 100 korona	1.0900	.900	0.9802	$ 334	$ 341	1.8%
2.	Austrian 100 corona	1.0900	.900	0.9802	335	342	2.1
3.	Krugerrand	1.0909	.916	1.0000	342	342	2.1
4.	Kilo bar (Engelhard)	32.1500	.999	32.1500	11,027	343	2.4
5.	1 ounce bar (Engelhard)	1.0000	.999	1.0000	349	349	4.2
6.	US medallion	1.1110	.900	1.0000	350	350	4.5
7.	Harwood (Gold Standard Corp.)	1.1200	.900	1.0000	351	351	4.8
8.	Mexican 50 peso	1.3400	.900	1.2057	425	352	5.1
9.	Maple leaf	1.0000	.999	1.0000	353	353	5.4
10.	Angel	1.0909	.916	1.0000	355	355	6.0
11.	Panda	1.0000	.999	1.0000	367	367	9.6
12.	British sovereign (old & new)	0.2568	.916	0.2354	87	370	10.5
13.	$20 double eagle (St. Gaudens, uncirculated)	1.0750	.900	0.9675	665	687	105.1

16. The best buy for silver bullion

Unlike the kilo bar in the gold market, when it comes to buying silver, you get the best deal when you buy the largest quantity. The absolute, bottom line best way to get the most silver for your money, buying retail, is to buy the 1000-ounce bar. Compared, for example, with buying the Mexican one-ounce libertad silver coins, you will get 22.8% more silver by buying 1000-ounce Sunshine bars. On a $10,000 investment, the difference amounts to a huge 343 extra ounces of silver.

This may sound like a paradox, but there is a compelling reason why you should <u>not</u> buy a 1000 ounce bar, even though it's clearly the best way to get the most silver for your dollars. The reason is simple -- they are so heavy (68.95 lbs.) and so awkward to carry (if you drop it you have a broken foot), and so hard to ship or store. Finally, if you want to pull a few thousand dollars out, you have to sell the whole bar, which isn't that easy because the retailers don't like them for the same reasons we don't. So we normally pay an extra dime an ounce and go to what we consider to be...

The best way to buy silver --
call Sunshine

Sunshine not only gave the best price on a 1000 ounce bar but also took the leading position in the investor-size 100-ounce silver bars. These conveniently sized bars have become a major factor in the retail silver market since they appeared on the scene in the late 1970s and early 1980s.

The Sunshine 100-ounce silver bars were priced at \$5.52 per ounce compared with the Engelhard at \$5.88, a savings of 36¢ an ounce or 6.5%. In between was the Royal Silver bar, a product of the Royal Canadian (government) Mint, that was priced at \$5.73 an ounce. There are a number of factors behind these price variations. The primary one is liquidity. The Engelhard bar is far better known than the others and is acceptable almost anywhere. There is a greater demand for it. Hence, they apparently can and do charge a higher price.

The Royal Silver 100-ounce bar has only been available for the past couple of years. These are the same folks who make the maple leaf gold coins, so their silver bars are

respected in the trade. But their silver products aren't yet good delivery on any futures exchange we know of, and it will take time for their silver bars to become well known with the investing public. Overall these bars provide an excellent buying opportunity offering a savings of 15¢ an ounce from the comparable Engelhard bars.

The major reason why the Sunshine bars are cheapest is because you're essentially dealing directly with the mining and refining company itself. You eliminate the middleman. Furthermore, if you should find some source that has a better price, call back to Sunshine. They guarantee to beat any retail-level price by anyone on nationally recognized hallmarks.

The best buy in one-ounce silver coins

There are also a large number of one ounce silver coins in wide distribution. These coins are issued by private companies, state and local governments, and anybody else who would like to commemorate anniversaries, honor individuals, or to celebrate various events. The premiums over spot range from around 15% (see the coins in this survey) to over 300% (MTB's liberty). We included five one ounce

silver coins in this survey. Their premiums over spot range from the Monex silver eagle of 14.4% over spot to A-Mark's liberty at 19.1% over spot.

The Monex one-ounce eagle seemed to have a unit price slightly lower than the Engelhard 100-ounce bar and the other one-ounce silver coins. But that is an unfair comparison because the eagles are sold in minimum lots of 250 coins (250 ounces). Logically, then, the 250 ounces of silver should sell for less than the Engelhard 100-ounce bar and the one-ounce silver coins, which they did. So the best buy among the one-ounce silver coins that you can buy in small quantities was -- once again -- Sunshine Bullion's product.

The worst silver bullion investment in our survey

Far and away the worst silver bullion investment in our survey was the one-ounce Mexican silver coin, the libertad, which carried what we believe to be an excessive 30% premium over spot. This is a semi-numismatic premium, but the current issues to the best of our knowledge have no reasonable expectation of ever gaining any numismatic

value. They are strictly bullion units. We buy a few each year because they are attractive. Another valid reason for buying them is because they are legal tender and in some states, this allows you to avoid sales tax.

The premiums of 14 popular silver investments

Rank	(Spot Silver $5.13/Troy Ounce) Unit[1]	Price Per Item	Price Per Unit ($/Troy oz.)	Percent Over Spot Price
1.	1000 oz. bar (Sunshine)	$5420.00	$5.42	5.7%
2.	1000 oz. bar (Engelhard)	5470.00	5.47	6.6
3.	100 oz. bar (Sunshine)	552.00	5.52	7.6
4.	100 oz. bar (Royal Can. Mint)	573.00	5.73	11.7
5.	100 oz. bar (Engelhard)	588.00	5.88	14.6
6.	Silver Eagle (Monex)	5.87	5.87	14.4
7.	Sunshine	5.98	5.98	16.6
8.	Harwood[2] (Gold Standard Corp.)	6.09	6.09	18.7
9.	Liberty (A-Mark)	6.11	6.11	19.1
10.	$1000 face value pre-1965 bag of US silver coins[3]	4440.00	6.21	21.1
11.	10 oz. bar (Engelhard)	63.34	6.34	23.6
12.	Prospector (Engelhard)	6.35	6.35	23.8
13.	1 oz. bar (Engelhard)	6.51	6.51	27.0
14	Libertad	6.66	6.66	30.0

1. All units are one ounce or a decimal multiple of .999 pure silver with the exception of footnoted units.
2. Total weight is 1.1154 troy ounce of .900 silver in an alloy of 90% silver and 10% copper that, when melted and refined, would produce one ounce of .999-fine silver.
3. Approximately 715 ounces per $1000 face value bag when melted and refined into .999-fine silver.

17. Two-tier market in Engelhard bars

When we did our sell-back survey we discovered a new development in 100-ounce silver bar quotes that could result in comparing apples to oranges. Although we were careful to specify in each call that we had an Engelhard brand 100-ounce silver bar -- in case prices might vary among different hallmarks -- we discovered that some dealers had a two-tier market for Engelhard bars. The reason for this is because Engelhard is marketing a new type of bar that commands a higher price with some dealers.

For years silver bars have been poured or "cast" by their fabricators. This type of fabrication rarely results in a bar that weighs exactly 100 ounces (the problem is magnified even more than the 1000-ounce bars), which is why the exact weight is stamped on each bar. In addition, the cast bars were somewhat drab and unattractive.

But since we did our last survey, Engelhard (and some other refiners) began making silver bars by an extrusion process. These 100-ounce extruded bars are infinitely more attractive. They are bright and shiny and come packaged in a plastic case. In addition, they are generally 100 ounces, although some grinding down at the refinery is necessary to bring them to the exact weight. For all these reasons, we

prefer the extruded bars to the cast ones.

Apparently the demand for these new "extruded" bars is great enough that some dealers are willing to pay a premium for them over their prices for the old cast bars. We found the premium in some cases to be as much as 15¢ an ounce. Other dealers, such as Sam Sloat, say the premium is unwarranted. Says Sam, "Silver's silver -- the bars all melt down to the same stuff."

Nonetheless you should be aware that some dealers have this two-tier market for Engelhard bars. This is because if you have one of the old cast Engelhard bars and fail to tell them so, they may give you the higher price. The discrepancy could throw off your own comparison shopping efforts, and you wouldn't find out about it until you shipped the bar to the dealer and receive a check for $15 less than you anticipated.

The bottom line is that if you wish to buy or sell silver bars, be sure that you specify in advance either cast or extruded bars. Doing this could save you the time and hassle of subsequent arguements over confusion between silver apples and oranges.

18. One danger in buying bullion

Some of the dealers sell their own name-brand bars of silver and gold. Most of these are not "good delivery" on a major exchange and normally sell at a discount. This discount would likely increase if that dealer went out of business.

Be sure you insist on a good delivery hallmark, such as Engelhard, Johnson Matthey, or Sunshine, whenever you buy silver and gold bullion.

19. US pre-1965 silver coins now a good buy for core holdings

We included a bag of $1000 face value pre-1965 US silver coins (halves, quarters, dimes) to see how they rate as a possible way to invest in silver bullion. The answer -- not that hot. Each of the bags contains approximately 715 ounces of .999 pure silver (on average if melted and refined). At the time of our survey, the unit price of the silver in bag form was 21.1% above spot.

There are two ways to look at buying bags of silver coins. Since you're buying over 700 ounces of silver, you should be getting a unit price quite comparable to 1000 ounce bars or 5.7%, instead of 21.1%. Secondly, in order to get the silver from coin form to .999 silver, you'd have to pay for the refinery charges thus adding even more to your per ounce unit price.

On the other hand, US silver coins are excellent for your core holdings of silver because of their near universal recognition. Looking at them from the standpoint of being able to buy small units of silver, such as dimes, for potential buying purposes during a possible breakdown in the currency system, bags of US silver coins are priced today at what we consider to be a bargain, and we recommend

them for that purpose.

While we do not recommend bags of US silver coins as bullion holdings, they still proved to be a better way to invest in silver bullion than three Engelhard products: their 10-ounce bar (23.6% above spot); their one-ounce silver coin, the prospector (23.8% above spot); and their one-ounce silver bar at a whopping 27% over spot.

One reason for the relatively high premiums on the one and 10-ounce silver bars is because of their serial numbers. Their market price says, in effect, that people are willing to pay more for this identification feature that could prove useful in case of theft, both for recovery and for insurance claims. If that's important to you, fine. But if you're only interested in buying the most silver for your dollars, they aren't the answer by a long shot.

Part III: How to buy and sell like an expert

20. Four guidelines that will help you save big dollars every time you buy or sell

To get the most mileage out of this survey, you should follow these 4 guidelines:

1. When you go to buy or sell, by all means call the three or four dealers that gave us the overall best prices. But you should also go to the tables where we've listed prices for individual investments. Sometimes a dealer has a speciality on a particular type of investment and can give you a bargain. The tables will reveal that.

2. If you buy or sell a second time, don't automatically assume that the dealer who gave you the best price last time will have the best price again. Recheck the prices on 3 or 4 dealers.

For example, Republic Bullion has traditionally been one of the best-priced dealers in our survey. However, on one day, the salesperson quoted a price on US silver coins (pre-1965) that was nearly $700 greater than the day before. If you had bought from them the first day, you would have had a great price. If you came back

on the second day, you would have gotten a terrible price.

3. See if your regular dealer will match -- or beat -- another dealer's price. Most people -- ourselves included -- have favorite dealers. Sometimes, they won't come in with the best price. Give your favorite dealer a chance to match it.

Let's face it, if you have an established relationship with a dealer, they won't want to lose your business.

For example, last year, when one of our callers told North American (now Norcap) that she'd like to shop around before she made a deal, the broker said, "Let me know what the other dealers quote you. I can't give you a guarantee, but I'll try to match it." That's the kind of opportunity you have to take advantage of.

4. If you buy or sell investments that aren't listed in the survey, use your head and your telephone.

A great example: As we were putting this Report to bed, we got an ad from Blanchard touting 1985 proof Canadian silver dollars: "Your last chance to own these stunning coins at low, issue prices: As low as $14.25 ea.!" exclaimed the ad: They were selling lots

of 20-100 coins at $14.95 apiece; lots of 101-500 at $14.75 each; 501-1,000 at $14.50 each; and 1,001 or more for $14.25 each.

We purchased the coins ourselves from the Canadian Mint to see what it would cost to buy 1 or 100 of them. They cost us only $12.87 per coin! On 100 coins you could save $295 -- from Blanchard's "low, issue price." You could use that $295 to buy another 24 proof silver dollars from the Canadian Mint.

21. Learn how to spot good deals -- and avoid rotten ones -- on your own

How to price out coins not covered in this survey

We covered all the main silver and gold bullion investments in this survey. But, if your mail looks anything like ours, you're probably being bombarded with ads selling a wide variety of other silver and gold coins.

Some of the deals offered are excellent. Alas, the great bulk of them seem truly rotten. We can't check them all out for you. You have to do that yourself. But how?

Calculating the premium over spot for silver and gold units

The key to intelligent price comparisons in bullion investments, of course, is to reduce all of the investment

units to a common denominator -- the price per troy ounce. Calculating the premium over spot then help put price differences into perspective.

The first step in calculating the premium of an investment is to divide the selling price by the number of pure silver or gold. That gives you the cost per troy ounce.

EXAMPLE: A bag of pre-1965 US silver coins ($1000 face value) contains approximately 715 troy ounces of pure silver. To calculate the cost per ounce, divide the selling price $4440 by 715, and you have the price of silver at $6.21 per ounce.

EXAMPLE: A Hungarian 100 korona contains 0.9802 troy ounces of pure gold. The selling price ($334) divided by 0.9802 gives you the price per ounce of pure gold = $340.75.

The next step in calculating the premium is to subtract the spot price from the cost per ounce; divide the remainder by the spot price; and convert to a percentage. To express this algebraically, the formula reads...

$$\text{Premium} = \frac{(\text{cost per ounce} - \text{spot price}) \times 100}{(\text{spot price})}$$

Once you have this nifty little formula, you can have all sorts of fun sniffing out rotten investment offers on your own.

22. How to buy silver and gold coins direct from a major wholesaler

On large purchases of silver and gold coins, you can buy direct from a major wholesaler, and get the same price as regular dealers like Investment Rarities or Deak. This is NOT one of the phony "at spot" or "wholesale" ads you've seen in the paper. It's for real.

If you want to buy in very large quantities, you can do it through Mocatta Metals, the giant silver and gold wholesaler. The minimum quantities you can purchase are...GOLD COINS: 100 ounces and up, US SILVER COINS: five bags (each of $1,000 face value) and up.

We did a quick price check on 100 maple leafs to make sure this would indeed mean savings to you. It did. The savings varied between $3 and $15 per maple leaf -- quite a lot on such a large purchase.

Mocatta is _not_ set up to service normal retail accounts. They aren't going to give you advice, try to help you make a decision, or give any other brokerage-type service. If you have questions such as "Should I buy?" "When should I buy?" or "What should I buy?" _don't call them_.

But, if you know exactly what you want to do and are prepared to call up and say, "I want to buy 100 maple leafs, what is your price," they'll take your order. They require 15% in good funds, in advance, before they will lock in a price. This can be done by bank wire, cashiers check, or certified check. When the check clears, they'll quote you a firm price.

23. How to buy silver and gold bullion the same way as major industrial users

If you want to buy VERY large quantities of silver or gold bullion (as opposed to coins), by far the cheapest way is to buy the nearest futures contract and take delivery of it. Silver, for instance, is generally just pennies more than the actual spot price in the cash market. The commission should run you between $40 and $100 -- well less than 10¢ per ounce of silver.

The minimum purchase on Comex is 5,000 ounces of silver or 100 ounces of gold. The minimum purchase on the Chicago Board of Trade (CBT) is 1,000 ounces of silver or a kilo bar of gold (32.15 ounces). The gold is in the form of 100-ounce or kilo bars; the silver is in the form of 1,000-ounce bars.

When you take delivery, you receive a warehouse receipt. We strongly recommend you leave the silver and gold in the warehouse. The reasons are:

(A) These exchange-approved depositories are about as safe a form of third-party storage as you're likely to find anywhere.

(B) The storage charge is minor.

(C) Buying like this leaves you in an excellent position to resell whenever you wish. You simply short the market and deliver the warehouse receipt to your broker. There's no fuss or delay about weight or hallmark. No assay charge. Indeed, it's almost like selling a share of stock -- that simple.

<u>If you want to keep your silver and gold at hand, these large bars of bullion are definitely NOT the best way to go</u>. They are white elephants on the investor market. Most dealers will not want to buy them from you unless you have them shipped directly from the warehouse. They're too easy to counterfeit. So, you'll very likely run into certification and assay charges when you do find a dealer who's willing to buy.

24. The only two methods that provide complete safety when you buy silver and gold

Deak & Co., Johnson Matthey, and Bullion Reserve proved that even the largest, most reputable dealers and wholesalers can get into financial trouble. We can't guarantee the financial security of any of the firms listed.

Even if you spend weeks checking out a dealer's reliability, there are really only two ways to buy silver and gold that provide complete protection against dealer default or bankruptcy: cash-and-carry purchase and sight drafts.

The sight draft is an excellent way to buy silver and gold. The dealer sends your silver and gold to your banker. You inspect the shipment. When you're satisfied that it's exactly what you ordered, you release the funds. The banker then wires your payment to the dealer and simultaneously releases the silver and gold to you. Both you and the dealer are fully protected every step of the way.

Unfortunately, many dealers would rather not provide sight drafts. They involve a lot of extra paperwork, time, trouble, and the dealer has to buy the metal before he gets your money. Furthermore, there is often a minimum purchase requirement or a fee for the service.

Which dealers offer sight drafts?

Dealer	Sight drafts offered?	Minimum	Fee
Auric	No		
Benham	No		
Blanchard	Yes	$5,000	none
Camino	Yes	none	none
Citibank	No		
Colonial	Yes, gold only	100 ounces	none
Deak-Perera	No		
First National Monetary	Yes	10 ounces	none
Fiscal & Monetary Services	Yes	silver: 100 oz. gold: 5 oz.	over $50,000 requires a 20% deposit
Gold Standard Corp.	Yes	none	1% of transaction
Harrison	No		
IPMC	Yes	$10,000	25% deposit
Investment Rarities	Yes	$10,000	20% deposit
Lee Numismatics	Yes	numismatics: none bullion: $1,500	bullion: $50 charge
Manfra, Tordella & Brookes	Yes	$2,000	none
Medlar's	Yes	none	inquire
Monex	No*		
Newcastle	Yes	none	none
Norcap	Yes	none	$20
Republic	No		
C. Rhyne	Yes	none	$40
Sam Sloat	No		
Security Rare Coins	Yes	silver: 100 oz. gold: 5 oz.	none
Shearson	No		
Silver Towne	Yes	none	none
Sunshine	Yes	500 oz.	$25
Western Federal	Yes	none	5% deposit required
Western Monetary	Yes	none	$10

*Monex *does* offer a bank custodial program that, to us, appears to also provide good safeguards. See our remarks under individual dealers for more details.

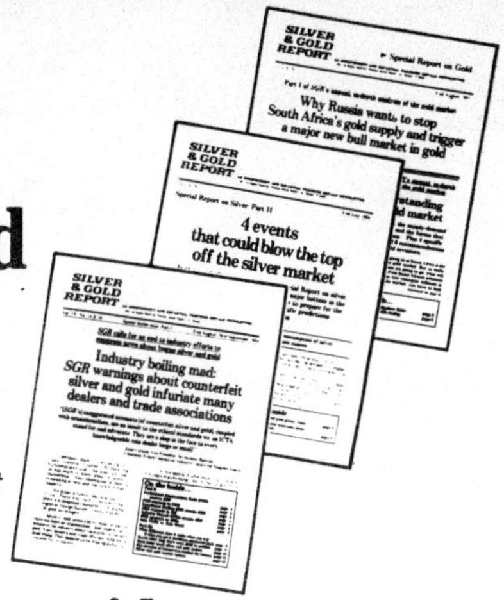

"Nobody has more accurately predicted movements in precious metals prices than Daniel Rosenthal..." —**Bill Ulrich, Publisher** ***Financial Security Alert***

"When I first met your Editor, I thought he was a nut! Then I started seeing things happen just as he said they would. So I started paying attention—and he has made me a bundle of money." —**L.R., New York, NY**

The SILVER & GOLD REPORT is NOT a dealer. We are NOT affiliated with any silver and gold dealer. We do NOT sell metals. We never have and never will. We DON'T get commissions, kickbacks, rebates, or remuneration of any kind from any dealer for their sales of metal. That leaves us totally free to call the shots -- bullish or bearish -- as we see them.

Furthermore, our independence allows us to specialize in showing investors how to avoid the traps, pitfalls, scams, and frauds that abound in the silver and gold industry.

For example, if your junk mail is anything like ours, you probably get endless dealer advertisements telling you the glories of one silver and gold investment or another. BUT THOSE ADVERTISEMENTS DON'T TELL YOU ABOUT THE SHORTCOMINGS.

Only the SILVER & GOLD REPORT analyzes all the major gold and silver investments (and some little-known ones, as well), and spells out, very specifically, the NEGATIVES as well as the positives.

Very often we steer readers away from very popular, but really ROTTEN high commission investments into superb, LOW COMMISSION INVESTMENTS WITH GREAT PROFIT POTENTIAL.

Furthermore, unlike other newsletters, the SILVER & GOLD REPORT does NOT stop after it tells you to buy or sell. Of all the newsletters out there covering silver and gold ONLY the SILVER & GOLD REPORT closely monitors the dealers -- gives you our recommendations on HOW to buy economically...WHAT silver and gold investments give you the best return on your money...and WHICH we believe are the safe (and fairly priced) dealers.

SILVER & GOLD REPORT, Daniel Rosenthal Editor:
One year, $144. Two years, $258.

"Anyone who buys silver or gold without reading your 'Insider's Guide' is crazy."

—Dick Young, Publisher
Young's World Money Forecast

"The most useful hard-money investing tool ever published" **—David Beare, Chairman International Trading Group**

"We've accumulated dozens upon dozens of valuable, nitty-gritty tips, hints, angles, and techniques for saving and making money on your silver and gold investments -- 3 years of investigative research -- into a massive Report titled, the "Insider's Guide to Buying Silver & Gold." Here, for instance, are just a few of the topics you'll read about...

- How to get an extra 15.9 ounces of pure silver for every 100 you buy. The premium over bullion on various silver investments varies widely. The Guide shows you the "best buys."

- How to get your money out of the country quickly, anonymously, with no reporting requirements, and absolutely legally. (Also: How to get it back into the country, when you do want it here).

- How to buy silver and gold the same way as industrial users and major dealers -- and save significant amounts on even modest-sized purchases.

- How to negotiate discounts with your regular dealer.

- The "obvious" -- but often overlooked -- mistake many investors make when opening a safe-deposit box.

- How to get your silver, gold, or cash out from a dealer who's withholding from you.

- 13 ways to help avoid getting taken by dealer default or fraud.

- A well-advertised offer we advise you should avoid at all costs.

Loren Biser, Editor of HEALTHVIEW NEWSLETTER, writes...

"Anyone ignoring the 'Insider's Guide' is asking -- no begging -- to get burned...fried...sizzled. We're not talking about buying something and losing a few dollars if the price goes down. We're talking about sinking thousands of hard earned dollars into something and simply not getting it -- ever."

"The Insider's Guide to Buying Silver & Gold," by Daniel Rosenthal: $78

"Why I turned bullish on gold after 2 years as a bear!"

—Daniel Rosenthal, Editor
Silver & Gold Report

The greatest bear market in gold in modern history is over.

4 powerful bullish forces are converging on the gold market: The destabilization of South Africa...the bank crisis...the plunging dollar...and a whiff of renewed inflation in the air. MUCH higher gold prices seem almost inevitable.

We have just published a Special Situation Report, "A Short Course in Gold Investing: The investor's guide to achieving financial security and independence." This Special Situation Report will help you take advantage of the new bull market to build independence and wealth with gold.

You'll learn the 3 most important reasons for owning gold... and how to choose gold investments that are best suited to each. For example, some gold investments offer superb -- but highly-leveraged -- profits that are great for an aggressive portfolio. But they are a disaster as core holdings. Other gold investments are wonderful as core holdings because they'll always be thought of as money. But these would fall flat on their faces in a speculative portfolio.

Other insights you'll read about are...

- How the international bank crisis is beginning to drive the gold market -- and the outlook for the near future.
- How the value of the dollar relates to gold prices.
- Why some investors should diversify with gold holdings outside the country. How to do it safely and privately.
- How to accumulate your weight in gold on a modest budget. Gold doesn't have to be "for the rich only." On this program you can accumulate a fortune, without going into debt to pay for it.
- Why both inflation and deflation are bullish for gold.
- How to avoid the traps and pitfalls when investing in gold.

"A Short Course in Gold Investing: The investor's guide to achieving financial security and independence," by Daniel Rosenthal and Ellen Young: $49.95.

"The dollar is finished. Kaput. It will be wiped out!"

--Dr Franz Pick

In a massive Special Report, THE TRIUMPH OF GOLD, Dr. Franz Pick, the world-famous monetary expert warns...

"Only gold will protect you. But you must know what to do because the US government will crawl into every safe deposit box in the country to get at your gold."

Every time we publish an article or book by Dr. Pick, friends and enemies alike tell us "You're going to destroy yourself." "Why are you publishing such garbage?" "He's NUTS." That's the measure of CONTEMPT Dr. Pick is held here in America.

But overseas -- in South America, Asia, and Europe -- it's the EXACT OPPOSITE. Before he retired, big muck-a-mucks in business and government paid him HUGE SUMS of money in personal consulting fees. Corporate presidents, treasurers, central bankers -- they all went to him for advice on the dollar crisis.

Why? Because THEY'VE gone through the wringer. THEY KNOW he speaks the truth. THEY KNOW he can help them avoid personal, corporate, and national calamity.

"The Triumph of Gold" is pure dynamite! It is NOT pleasant reading. What Dr. Pick tells you about the future of the dollar -- and how it will affect your business and personal finances -- will probably infuriate and upset you. But you'll see how your dollars are being destroyed, and what you can do to protect yourself.

Here in America, we think bad inflations and currency collapses are calamites that happen only to other people in other countries. That's the SINGLE WORST INVESTMENT MISTAKE you can make.

There's no need to put yourself at risk like that. There's no need to worry about going to bed well-to-do (or rich) one evening, and waking up trapped, DEAD BROKE the next morning. Do what I do for my friends and mom. Take 15% to 20% of your portfolio and invest it along Dr. Pick's recommendations.

THE TRIUMPH OF GOLD will make the difference between YOU (and your family) going through the wringer with the rest of them, or coming out intact, unscathed -- while the rest of the country groans in financial agony.

"The Triumph of Gold," by Dr. Franz Pick: $92.

"If every precious metals investor had read this, not one penny would have been lost in the IGBE or Bullion Reserve scandals."

—Howard Ruff, Editor
Financial Success Report

Back in May and June of '82, SGR examined 8 gold and silver dealers we had heard rumors about. SGR gave 2 of the dealers clean bills of health; the other 6 SGR publicly warned against.

Of the 2 dealers to which we gave clean bills of health, both are around today, happy and prosperous. Of the 6 we warned against, every single one is now out of business. Total casualties: Over 30,000 investors lost some $80 million to $100 million.

It was the same thing with Bullion Reserve. Outside of Howard Ruff and SGR, everybody thought they were legitimate. We published blistering warnings and our subscribers got out safe and sound. Unfortunately, over 20,000 nonsubscribers were burned to the tune of $59 million.

The problem is worse, today. There seem to be more sleazy and ruthless dealers out there than ever before. Our research files are bulging. We can't possibly check them all out. We don't have the resources. And even if we did, there are so many of them they would crowd everything else out of SGR. We'd never have enough space for a market analysis or investment recommendation.

So you need "something" that will help you steer clear of the not-so-clean or shaky dealers. This "Investors Checklist" was written expressly to fill that need -- to help you buy gold and silver safely. The questions in the "Checklist" are the same basic questions that enabled us to see through IGBE, Bullion Reserve, and Premex. These are the questions that enabled us to see the problems in those firms and warn investors away before it was too late.

Included are extensive notes to explain the significance of your dealers' answer, so you can spot the red flags immediately.

"Silver & Gold Investor's Checklist:
What to ask dealers before you buy (or sell),"
by Daniel Rosenthal: $49.95.

"Silver and gold dealers tried to put me out of business before I could publish this book."

—Daniel Rosenthal, Editor
Silver & Gold Report

Some of the dealers hated our articles on counterfeit silver and gold so much that they ganged up to try to put us out of business before we could publish this book. But we got the inside documents, published them, and blew the whistle on the plot.

"Counterfeit Silver & Gold: How to spot and avoid it" gives you the facts about counterfeits that the dealers would almost kill to keep from you. Such as...

- 5 warning signs that you may already have counterfeit gold in your portfolio.
- The hidden trap in dealer guarantees.
- Why counterfeiters LOVE gold coin jewelry.
- A 5-second density test that enables you to spot all known varieties of counterfeit maple leafs and other major bullion coins.
- 7 suggested dealers for purchasing semi-numismatic silver and gold coins.

Listen, gold prices are going to boom. You can be wallowing in profits in a few years. I'd hate to see you lose out because you got some of the millions of counterfeit gold coins in circulation today.

SO DON'T GET STUCK WITH WORTHLESS COUNTERFEITS LIKE THESE

The guidelines in "Counterfeit Silver & Gold: How to spot and avoid it" show you where the main dangers are -- and how to avoid them. These are the same steps we take when we buy for ourselves and for friends.

"Counterfeit Silver & Gold: How to spot and avoid it," by Daniel Rosenthal and Ellen Young: $69.

"Oh my God! My gold is *gone*!"

Imagine coming home from work one evening and finding a telegram from your bank or warehouse...your safe deposit box was robbed. Or seeing that your home was burglarized -- and your gold is gone. Your core holdings -- the stores you set aside for financial independence -- everything you worked at for so many years has been WIPED OUT.

> It's so scary you don't even want to think about it. But it's already happened to hundreds of other silver and gold investors.

Most people think they can put their gold in a bank or private safe deposit box, and it's "safe." They put it in, and sit back -- until catastrophe strikes.

For example, Chris Weber tells of the horror faced by customers of Swiss Security Vaults in Denver...

> "In August of 1982, Swiss Security Vaults... was violated. The alarm system wasn't on, and only four small bolts needed to be removed to gain access. It is still not clear whether it was an inside job. What is certain is that 150 boxes were pried open; well over $1 million was looted...Moreover, the insurance company denied all boxholder claims, for over two years."

Later, he tells of break-ins to three bank vaults, United California Bank (now First Interstate), Chase Manhatten, and Crocker International. In all three cases, the bank denied liability. The investors learned too late, that banks do NOT insure their customer's safe deposit boxes.

There's no reason you should put yourself at this kind of risk. Chris Weber has compiled a superb Report, The "Guide to Safe Storage of Silver & Gold." It's the ONLY Report on the subject available and a must for every silver and gold investor -- whether you store your silver and gold at home, in a bank, or at a private warehouse.

"Chris Weber's Complete Guide to Safe Storage of Silver & Gold," by Chris Weber: $68

Take all your books on silver and HEAVE them into the East River

All those books on silver you have around the house are hopelessly out of date. That's why 98% of the people who've bought silver in the past 5 years are LOSING MONEY.

The problem is this: There's been a fundamental change in the silver market. It began on January 21, 1980, when silver prices peaked at $48 an ounce. It's now complete. Nearly everybody has missed it. Your strategy for investing in silver is probably based on old information. It doesn't work anymore. Your books on silver are out of date.

"The New Case for Silver" will show you how to stop the losses and start the profits again. You'll learn...

* 4 errors almost all investors make about silver.

* 12 powerful reasons why I look for silver prices to rise steeply.

* The ONLY silver investment that hedges against BOTH inflation and deflation. This overlooked US silver coin investment offers you outstanding profit potential with sharply limited risk.

* Powerful leverage in silver, with complete protection against margin calls and forced liquidations. Sound too good to be true? Well, it isn't. It exists and it's perfect for investors who seek huge, speculative profits and are willing to accept corresponding risks.

* Our choice for the best, safest way to turn US dollars into Swiss silver. It's not a Swiss bank. Title is in your name. It's insured, moderately priced, and there's no reporting requirement.

* 4 events that could blow the top off the silver market.

There is no reason on earth you have to make the same, identical mistakes that tens of thousands of other silver investors are making. It is now completely up to you whether or not you're going to stop losing money in silver -- and start making it. Give yourself a break. STOP INVESTING ON OLD, OUT-OF-DATE INFORMATION ABOUT THE SILVER MARKET.

"The New Case for Silver,"
by Daniel Rosenthal and Ellen Young. $82.

ORDER FORM

How to get in on the ground floor of the silver and gold markets—with information most people don't have

☐ **Learn the traps, pitfalls, and frauds in the silver and gold industry.** The *Silver & Gold Report* is NOT a dealer. We're not affiliated with any dealer. That leaves us totally free to call the shots—about the market, dealers, and investments—as we see them.

☐ Two year subscription, $258.

☐ One year subscription, $144.

☐ **Get out of rotten, high-commission investments and into superb, low-commission investments.** The "Insider's Guide to Buying Silver & Gold" contains dozens upon dozens of valuable, nitty-gritty hints, tips, angles, and techniques for saving and making money in your silver and gold investments. By Daniel Rosenthal: $78.

☐ **Why I turned bullish after 2 years as a bear.** "A Short Course in Gold Investing: The investor's guide to achieving financial security and independence" will show you the 3 most important reasons for buying gold and how to buy the right gold investments for your needs. By Daniel Rosenthal and Ellen Young: $49.95.

☐ **"The dollar is finished. Kaput. It will be wiped out,"** warns Dr. Franz Pick in his last great work, "The Triumph of Gold." Learn how to preserve your wealth while all paper monies fail. By Dr. Franz Pick: $92.

☐ **"If every investor had read this, not one penny would have been lost in the IGBE or Bullion Reserve scandals."**—Howard Ruff, Editor, *Financial Success Report.* "The Silver & Gold Investor's Checklist: What to ask dealers before you buy (or sell)" will help you avoid losing thousands of dollars in a dealer fraud or default. By Daniel Rosenthal: $49.95.

☐ **They tried to put us out of business before we could publish this book.** "Counterfeit Silver & Gold: How to spot and avoid it" shows the main dangers in buying gold and how to avoid them. The same steps we take when buying for ourselves and our friends. By Daniel Rosenthal and Ellen Young: $69.

☐ **Don't lose your gold to a burglar or fraudulent private warehouser.** The "Complete Guide to Safe Storage of Silver & Gold" will show you how to store your silver and gold **safely** and **privately.** By Chris Weber: $68.

☐ **Stop losing money in silver and start making it again.** "The New Case for Silver" will show you why 98% of the people who bought silver in the past 5 years have LOST MONEY—and why you DON'T have to be one of them. By Daniel Rosenthal and Ellen Young: $82.

☐ **Complete set, $488.90:** 7 books filled with information you cannot get anywhere else. You get a one year subscription to the *Silver & Gold Report* as a **free bonus.** Total savings: $144.

Please return entire order form

My total order comes to $ ______________________

☐ My check or money order is enclosed

Please charge my ☐ VISA ☐ MasterCard

Acct. # ______________________ Exp. Date __________

Signature ______________________

Name ______________________

Address ______________________

City ______________________

State ______________________ Zip __________

IPG 1

The Institute for the Preservation of Wealth, Inc.
P.O. Box 40, Bethel, CT 06801